THE
ULCER DIET
COOK BOOK

by HAROLD RUBIN

with an Introduction by
FRANZ J. LUST, M.D., L.F.A.C.G.
Past President, New York Academy of Gastroenterology

Published by
M. EVANS AND COMPANY, INC., New York
and distributed in association with
J. B. LIPPINCOTT COMPANY,
Philadelphia and New York

Library of Congress Catalog Card Number: 63-9769
Manufactured in the United States of America

Designed by James Darby

To all my friends for their patience during a trying period; and especially to R. K. for his kind aid, and to F. and C. S. for their encouragement.

v

CONTENTS

INTRODUCTION

Since you are reading this book, it is safe to assume that your doctor has either told you that you have an ulcer or — what is more likely, perhaps — that your husband has one. People respond to that diagnosis in different ways. To some it comes as an alarming shock. Others accept it almost gratefully as an understandable explanation of their symptoms. But for everyone it means a temporary change in their eating habits.

Ulcers have been with us for a long time. Medications of sorts were prescribed for them centuries ago and, particularly within the past three decades, many new ones have been put on the market. We can be sure that the future will produce its full quota. At least two or three times a year, on an average, there is a flurry in the press about some new discovery. Usually the announcement comes at a meeting of one of the large medical associations, but at any time an alert magazine or newspaper writer may chance upon a research story that can be made into exciting reading.

The wonder-pills come and go. It is true that a few useful ones continue to be prescribed, but within a year or so after their heralded appearance, most of them are completely forgotten. Still, your doctor expects to read about something "new" every three years — even though it is unlikely to be entirely new. His desk will be piled high once again with samples and with brochures and pamphlets relating the incredible success of the new concoction.

But no matter how many pills and powders, tablets and fluids there are available, the key to the successful treatment of an ulcer is diet. Nowadays diets of one kind or another seem to be extraordinarily fashionable. Some people seem to be perpetually on a diet, turning from one faddish method to another in an effort to find some pleasant (if ineffectual) way to reduce their girth and poundage. Occasionally, though much more rarely, one even encounters a person industriously consuming calories to gain weight. Most of these people can be as lax and casual about their dieting as they please. But you don't have their freedom. As an ulcer patient you *have* to diet to get well. There is no short-cut treatment for your ulcer, no miracle injection to rid you in a few days of the aches and pains forever. As you have undoubtedly discovered, it is necessary to adapt yourself to your ulcer in many ways. And whatever else is required, the change always involves the elimination of certain foods from your diet, either temporarily or for a longer period of time.

The usual ulcer diet is not an attractive one, and inevitably there arises the question of how you can adjust to it most easily, how you can avoid being repelled by the tastelessness and monotony of what you are required to eat. I have long made it a rule to discuss the prescribed diet not only with the patient but also with the person who prepares his food. Since the majority of ulcer victims are men, that means that I usually find it necessary to explain to their wives how to prepare ulcer-diet dishes. That seems to me an important step. It is not enough, I think, to give an ulcer patient a list which indicates what foods he may or may not eat, for the way the foods are prepared may also make a critical difference.

Even on a very restricted diet there are still, of course, many types of food which the ulcer patient may safely eat. But, particularly in the early stages, there are more that he may not have. And these vary, not only because of the differences in people, but also because the composition of the food itself may differ in various parts of the world. For example, certain kinds of meat which might be permitted in Europe are, in the form usually available in the United States, hard on the stomach. Some vegetables, which are generally acceptable, may be disturbingly gassy if they have been grown in particular types of soil or with certain kinds of fertilizers. Because of all these possible variations, I have found it most useful to discuss foods and cookery with the person who is to prepare my ulcer patient's meals. Happily, I think that it is relatively easy to handle these variations here in the United States where there is such a variety of foods available at all seasons — unless, of course, some strike or tie-up messes up the whole transportation system. And that, fortunately, does not happen more than once every few years or so.

The doctor tells his ulcer patient that he must stick to a "bland diet" and eat only light food. He gives him examples and perhaps a list. That may very well satisfy the patient himself, even though *bland* may have as many different definitions as the word *love*. But his wife immediately senses the problems she faces. "How," she asks, "am I to prepare meals with this diet?"

Generally, I am afraid, there is a long pause before the doctor answers. Chances are that he hasn't been in the kitchen much lately — unless you count those midnight visits to the refrigerator. He tries, in a vague sort of way, to answer as helpfully as he can, but both the patient's wife and the doctor soon realize that cookery was not stressed in the curriculum at medical school.

It is precisely at this point, I think, that Mr. Rubin's book should prove useful. He had an ulcer and he was bored with the food prescribed for his diet. But, being a non-professional cook, he didn't meekly resign himself to the tedium of an unpleasant diet. He decided to try to make the best of what he was permitted to eat. He must have experimented a great deal in his kitchen for he has much to say about the proper use of a skillet; about blenders (which will do much more than most people realize); about condiments that were strange to me at least. And I rather pride myself on my culinary knowledge, for in my bachelor days I prepared my own meals and in time became a passable cook — until, many years ago, my wife briskly took the job out of my hands.

But — I admit it gladly — Mr. Rubin's skills far surpass mine. He has developed dozens of interesting and varied ways to prepare simple, healthy food. And he has fancy concoctions in the book too — dishes that would enhance the repertoire of even a very skilled housewife. There are many combinations that I would never have thought of using had I not read Mr. Rubin's suggestions. Whoever wields the ladle and reigns in the kitchen will want to try these recipes. And change them, I suppose. For diet cooking means adapting foods to an individual's taste and the stage of his ulcer; and even a person who has an ulcer is still entitled to have his own likes and dislikes.

This book does not pretend to be a medical guide and should not, of course, be used as one. No book can be a substitute for a doctor's instructions. As I have already said, food that is wholesome and healthful for one ulcer sufferer may tend to upset the digestion of another. On page 31 you will find a list of the basic ingredients used in the recipes of this book. Show it to your doctor and ask him to make any changes or deletions that your particular condition may require. Your doctor is also the person to tell you when you may expect to move from the first phase of the diet to the next.

There are rows of diet books on library shelves, most of them written by doctors and home economics experts. This one is different. Its author is a fellow-sufferer who has been over the rough dietary road that all ulcer victims must travel. What he has done here is to devise ways that make it possible to diet — and enjoy it. I hope that his suggestions will shorten your way to a fine seven-course dinner (without diet, of course) topped off by a glass of ice cold, sparkling champagne. Prosit!

Franz J. Lust, M.D.

New York, N.Y.

THE ULCER DIET COOK BOOK

ABOUT GOOD FOOD AND ULCERS

I have a gastric ulcer — two of them, in fact, in different parts of the lining of my stomach. Under doctor's care, with medication, rest, and diet, they have been healed and lulled into dormancy. I would prefer to say that I have *had* ulcers, but I have been warned to treat them as they if they were still with me. So I say I *have* ulcers.

An ulcer means a diet — and at the beginning, often a drastically unpleasant one. Nobody takes kindly to a diet, and when whole categories of tempting foods are denied to the victim, and others which he can barely abide are thrust upon him a dozen times a day, food — or even talk about food — can easily become an abomination.

Some diets offer at least a sense of accomplishment. If you cut your caloric intake sufficiently to see that extra poundage melt away, your hunger pangs are to some degree alleviated as your girth diminishes. But an ulcer diet, especially in the early stages, is simply pleasureless. It is sharply restricted, endlessly repetitive — and fattening. Whole milk, cream, butter, and starches. Something *can* be done to make them more palatable. Indeed, a great deal can be done, as I hope this book will demonstrate. But however imaginatively you combine those early-ulcer elements, you cannot reduce their caloric content. You simply have to face this unpleasant fact with whatever equanimity you can muster, and then go on from there to make the best of what is clearly a bad situation.

A person who is by nature indifferent to food, may think that he can adjust to an ulcer regime with less difficulty than those of us who actively enjoy food and the pleasures of the bottle. I doubt that is really true. In my experience, indifferent eaters usually confine themselves to a relatively few favorite foods. They are not generally very open-minded about trying new foods, and when the old ones are forbidden, they are often acutely unhappy.

But so are those who have a broader range of tastes. I have always had more than a casual interest in food and cookery. The doctor's diagnosis sounded like doom itself. The program he outlined seemed a sentence to a lifetime without food, drink, or tobacco. It wasn't, of course, as catastrophic as that, but it sounded that way at the time.

The discovery of my ulcers had some unexpected consequences. In the usual time I recovered from the alarm-and-despair stage. But ambulatory illness of long duration, I found, tended to create an amazingly total absorption in the relatively simple problems of nourishment. Though I had been as casual about meal times as anyone — and a bit more, perhaps — I now found myself living by a metronome. I watched the clock from morning to night. Conscientiously I took the prescribed food at precisely the prescribed hour.

And I made endless conversation (I now realize) about my ulcers. There were details for sympathetic co-sufferers and excuses for disbelieving friends; there were symptoms, and worries, and explanations.

In time I realized that I was a member of the not-so-exclusive group of ulcer sufferers. My course of treatment had been settled, I was on my diet, and I accepted the fact that I was an ambulatory invalid.

I made light of this. Ulcers are an affliction with a stylish stigma. I have not been able to discover why ulcers are so generally socially acceptable. They are not necessarily a rich man's hobby, nor are they truly symptomatic of success. Women seem to have gotten them with the vote and equal rights. People in all walks of life, work, and background get them. They are not exclusively the badge of the executive, but ulcers, for some reason, do seem to convey an aura of strength rather than weakness.

That ulcers are rather difficult to conceal has both advantages and disadvantages. It should and does make it simple for the victim to insist on certain special privileges such as consideration in menu planning. But you also become fair game for every amateur diagnostician. Occasionally I was told, "Forget it." This is the simplest advice to ignore. Harder to shrug off were the well-meaning friends who insisted on dining with me. I learned to avoid this temptation because of variations on such gems as: "A little bit can't hurt you." "Just taste this." "Don't you wish you could eat . . ." "We all have to go sometime." "Is it worth it?" And, "Does it hurt?"

Considering how careful qualified physicians are in discussing the elusive causes and cures of ulcers, I was amazed at the number of people of my own acquaintance who could without hesitation prescribe *the miracle cure* — which almost invariably turns out to have worked its wonders for some person several persons removed from the teller of the tale.

I am not a physician and I won't give you medical advice. Perhaps it *is* true that strange medications, homilies, and exotic diets have worked marvelous cures. I only know that I thought it wisest to take my doctor's advice. After I had heard for the twentieth time how some nameless ulcer victim had been restored to perfect health overnight, I learned to anticipate my well-wishing friends, to explain flatly that my doctor had made his diagnosis, and that I was happy with the treatment and diet that he prescribed. Only occasionally, I found, was it necessary to raise my voice and insist that it was *my u*lcer we were discussing, not that of somebody else's friend, cousin, or uncle.

Try to keep your temper — but be sure you keep to your diet.

An ulcer will alter your gastronomical world. It will not obliterate it. You have food. You eat at home and dine away from home — and there are dangers in both places.

At home the temptations are the forbidden foods within easy reach. Away from home, taboo foods are often placed before you. Not only must you learn to say no; you must repeat it, and say it again. That "little bit of" will be discomfitting to you, not to the person who insists that you try it. You learn to be relentlessly logical. If the bland diet is helping you, you ask yourself, why prolong its necessity by going on and off the diet? You become an expert at saying no to all blandishments.

It is the theme of this book that an ulcer diet need not be an intolerable and prolonged succession of tasteless concoctions. With some knowledge of food, a dash of inventiveness, and a willingness to experiment a bit, you can plan a long range diet that you can follow with ease — and unlikely as it probably seems — one that from time to time will provide flashes of real pleasure.

Not, I hasten to add, from the first day. In my own case — and, I suppose, with most beginners — the advice left little latitude: have frequent medical examinations, get as much rest as possible, stop smoking, stay on the diet.

The first few days of that diet called for no great culinary skill. Fourteen times during a twenty-four hour period for three days I drank a mixture of sweet cream and milk in equal proportions. But there was solid matter too — pills and capsules.

From this regime I was promoted to eating and drinking thirteen times daily for seven more days. But at least there was variety. The milk-cream mixture alternated with cooked cereal, boiled or poached eggs, buttered toast, rice, puréed vegetables, and an occasional bit of boiled chicken, fish, lamb, or liver.

During this phase, too, I started eating prepared baby foods as a recommended short cut in preparing my meals. You don't, I assume, imagine that an infant's diet is a happy solution to the problem. It isn't. To the adult of sound tooth, the texture of baby food is not welcome. Nor from any aesthetic standpoint are the little jars pleasant; I especially objected to the grinning babies on the labels who seem to leer knowingly at you. Worse still, many of the mixtures are surprising combinations of ingredients you must avoid. Of course, there is no way of knowing what quantities are used. But hunger helps, and with diligence you may find simpler varieties that are more or less pleasant to the taste. In time you may even become so expert that you select your strained nourishment carefully from the brands on the grocery shelf.

Just about the time that you think your taste buds have been forever atrophied, the situation reverses itself. Or so it was with me. In the first place, you begin to feel better. A little later, the restrictions are loosened a trifle. Gingerly you experiment with morsels of favorite foods, hoping that you can report no ill effects. All goes well. The future returns.

There are few good things to be said for an ulcer diet. But there is at least one, and to me it came as a delightful surprise. I found that my sense of taste had been astonishingly heightened. Giving up tobacco, alcohol, and heavily spiced foods had restored my sense of smell to such a degree that I could easily appreciate the natural flavors of foods that had once seemed almost tasteless. The weeks of deprivation had actually revealed a whole new spectrum of taste sensations that I had been missing for years.

I have since learned that the experience is not at all uncommon, that many an ulcer patient has emerged from treatment not only cured, but also epicurean.

Encouraged by this new development, I again began to indulge my interest in cookery. With my doctor's permission, I began to experiment with new and unusual combinations of foods on the permitted list of my diet. That turned out to be more rewarding than I had hoped. Again I began to be interested in what I ate. My menu was far more varied. Best of all, the relaxation in the kitchen after a day's work proved to be excellent therapy.

As my repertoire grew and my interest in it increased, so the scope of my cooking activities expanded. I moved from trials with combinations of liquid foods to experiments with a more normal diet — still within strict limitations. Still later, I was permitted to broaden the range of the flavorings with which these semi-normal foods could be prepared. By careful planning and judicious selection, I found I could serve full meals. That was an achievement in itself. But what delighted me most was that some of my friends found that they actually enjoyed ulcer diet food.

About this time I stumbled on two facts which everyone who has had to prepare an ulcer diet meal soon discovers. The first was that the food, being rather special, turns out to be surprisingly expensive in terms of waste. Cooking and eating only the breast of the chicken, the eye of the chop, and the fillet of the steak leaves a lot of good food uneaten. I am not frugal, I think, but I have a streak of thrift, and the waste distressed me. I found that poaching an entire chicken and reserving most of the breast for myself was a sound investment. The broth and the rest of the meat could be used for making another dish and served to the non-dieters.

The second discovery came when the doctor lifted the ban on flavorings a bit more. I began to think of fresh herbs as a variety of vegetable. This notion proved to be useful. A sprig or two used instead of spice in cooking, and then discarded before the food was served, opened a new world of flavor to me. That miniscule pinch of salt could at least be enhanced with a taste of tarragon, basil, parsley, and several other herbs. Garlic, onions, and pepper were still a long way off, but after weeks without any extra stimulus to taste, even these few mild herbs were a marvelous treat. A drop or two of lemon juice produced real piquancy. Honey and maple sugar added a new dimension to sweetening.

A little taste of success stimulates effort, and from that point

forward my file of notes and menus and recipes grew with surprising rapidity.

It was that file that became the basis of this book.

PHASES AND STAGING

The preponderance of ulcer victims, I'm told, are men. They
have the pain and inconvenience, but it is their wives in most
cases who have the double chore of preparing diet foods for the
patient — foods that are as varied and tempting as the circumstances permit — and at the same time serving wholesome and
attractive meals to their family and guests. This book is intended
to help them with what is admittedly a difficult assignment.

You will see that the recipes have been labeled: *early phase*
and *later phase*. The early-phase foods may, of course, be eaten
by a person ready for those in the second group. Unhappily, the
reverse is not true. But this much can be said for even the first
phase dishes: I find that I have added many of them to my normal post-ulcer diet. I continue to enjoy them — and so do friends
at my table.

Even though the terms seem self-descriptive, it is perhaps
wise to define them rather specifically as they are used here.
Early Phase. The very cautious period that follows the strictly
liquid diet. Its duration will, of course, be determined by the
patient's doctor. This is the beginning of the diet as outlined
herein. It includes the first "solid" foods and the beginning of
home therapy under medical supervision.
Later Phase. The period after healing has shown signs of progress
and diet restrictions have been eased. Though the patient is still
under medical supervision, greater latitude is allowed in choosing
foods. Eating has begun to center more around meals and meal
times and less on food divided among so many feedings and
taken as medication. Of course, there is still the need to continue

drinking milk and having little snacks between meals, but these are becoming less important to patient, doctor, and ulcer.

Staging or *Preparation Staging* are terms that may need a little explanation. They are there simply as guidance for the person who is preparing the meal and only incidentally do they relate to the ulcer patient's diet. Staging is a guide to efficiency and economy in the kitchen.

Since the family need not (and should not) adopt a restricted ulcer diet as a program, the preparation of two meals instead of one can be burdensome. It needn't be, for the family can easily enjoy different dishes prepared from food that is permitted the ulcer patient. For example: You can poach an entire chicken and use only the white meat for the ulcer patient. The rest of the meat is diced and made into a curry. This is relatively quick and economical. It avoids waste and double cooking methods.

The same technique applies to vegetables. Cook sufficient for the entire family and purée only that amount necessary for the dieter's portion. Some of the recipes in this book will satisfy the needs of both the patient and the cook. Others may be prepared and divided, with each part finished with a minimum of additional effort for separate requirements. The tricks of method and timing I have called staging.

I have said that staging is intended only as an aid to the family cook. That may be understating its value – though here, I admit, I am trespassing in the doctor's field. It is surely safe to say, however, that a feeling of ease and harmony in the family may well contribute to the ulcer-healing process. It is also evident that the family unit in which a member must follow a special diet finds itself with a twofold problem: food budgets and "togetherness." The suggestions for *Preparation Staging* will help in both areas. The recipes and menus avoid the waste of costly foods. The completed recipes will put essentially the same foods on each plate, giving a unity to the meal.

Early in his diet the ulcer patient subsists on frequent, small feedings. During this period the sharing of meals with others is more a ritual than a necessity. Dinner will be only one more stop on a long day full of many similar stops. It will at least be some small comfort to all if the shared foods are not so radically different that the dieter feels painfully excluded.

How important staging will be to your patient and your family only you can decide. It depends largely on your understanding of the ulcer victim's tastes and personality. Will it be a minor source of anguish to him if one of his favorite foods is served at table while it is forbidden to him? Minor anguish, yes, but the ulcer patient's daily pattern is filled with a host of petty annoyances. The question deserves a thoughtful answer, and the solutions offered by the staging method should be of help.

DINING AWAY FROM HOME

Dining away from home poses its own problems. Personally, I preferred staying at home for as many meals as possible during my convalescence. Actually, I prefer my own hearth and table to those of others under most circumstances. Besides, it was difficult to suggest to a person kind enough to invite me to dinner that he should cook the foods I was permitted — and under my direction. At the same time, doing so was a necessity if I was not to retire from all socializing for an entire year.

I found that the easiest approach was to suggest simple basic foods such as broiled ground steak or chicken and a jar or two of baby food and milk. Always milk. Or I ate before leaving home and drank milk with my host. Or I asked for a poached egg and other safe fare.

Restaurants I avoided for a long time. When at last I did venture forth, I tried the ones with homey atmosphere and clean, simple home cooking. They were disaster. They allowed for "no substitutions" on their menus. There were surprisingly few foods for me to choose from and very little special preparation was allowed in their kitchens.

So I crossed restaurants off my list. Except for lunch counters. They remained because I discovered that there I could get my blender confections made in their malted milk machines. I must admit that I had these remarkable concoctions frequently, often to the horror of the person whipping them up. But if I reassured the attendant that I would eat what I asked him to prepare, he would usually make it.

Then one day I had to keep a business appointment in a restaurant at dinner time. As usual, I prepared for the occasion by eating earlier at home. The restaurant, one that serves good French cuisine, was a place I had often frequented in the past. Fortunately, I knew my business clients well, and I also knew the owner of the restaurant. My friends heard my story and commiserated properly.

The restaurateur, however, was determined that I have something to eat. So I ordered milk. This was even more painful to him. He drew a chair to the table and asked about my diet. He insisted that surely I could eat purée and beefsteak and many other things.

I agreed. But what of seasoning and cooked fats and the bother to the chef.

"There is no such thing as bother to a good chef; we prepare each dish to each person's order anyway. Let me get you the following . . ."

And I was returned to the gastronomical fold. From that day I found that honest French and Italian restaurants as well as steak houses and sea food places were my refuge. That is, provided they did actually prepare each dish for me and to my specific order. The permitted meats, fish, vegetables, pasta, and desserts could all be safely enjoyed. They were broiled, boiled, poached, and so on as I needed them. Spaghetti and butter, creme caramel, puréed spinach, a broiled fillet – they were all mine for the asking.

I know that this sounds snobbish and expensive. It need not be. Nearly everyone has favorite dining places where he is known to a waiter or to the owner. Start there, and lay your case before the help. If they truly care about food, they will comfort you with comestibles. Your own curiosity about what they can do may awaken the waiter from his apathy, from the air of indifference created (in good part, I think) by his customer's lack of real interest in food. I think you will be astonished at the solicitude and care that normally indifferent waiters will lavish on you.

SHOPPING FOR FOOD

For most ulcer patients shopping is only a minor problem. It was a little more difficult for me, for I do my own shopping, and when I began to wander through the supermarket with my list of permitted foods, I'm afraid that I spent most of my time gazing longingly at those I could not have. But that too passed.

In a reasonably well-stocked store you can get the fruits and vegetables you need – canned, frozen, or, in season, fresh. Since I could have little, I decided to have the best. Fresh, I thought. But fresh foods often turned out to be the poorest choice, since the problems of transportation from distant gardens to the shelves makes it necessary to pick food before it is at its best. By the time you get it, if it travels far, it is often neither fresh nor tasteful. As your palate becomes more sensitive, the question of taste will become increasingly important to you.

An honest butcher, like a good waiter, is a person worth cultivating assiduously. He will help you select cuts to avoid waste, and he is often very knowledgeable about cookery. I have always found that it is economical to pay a slightly higher price per pound for meat or fish that is cut to order and trimmed as you want it to be rather than to make do with those cellophane-wrapped packages at the special sale price.

A large market is usually the best place to shop. There you can see the variety of pasta shapes, each with its own taste, the many cereals, the fruits and vegetables at their seasonal best, the canned items. But take some time to study the labels and to learn about the ingredients in the food packages. Is this jelly safe or that prepared pudding mix? It's worth the trouble to look for new packaged foods that will save you hours of preparation time in the kitchen.

AFTER THE ULCER

How long you must abide by your diet and how stringent it must be only your doctor can tell you. But somewhere ahead of you lies recovery — and I can only hope that yours will be as complete as mine has been.

One by one I re-introduced certain foods to my diet, slowly, carefully, and in small quantities. I suppose you will progress in the same fashion. I did not eat two or three strange dishes at one meal and then wonder which might have upset me. I found that the taste for spice in excess is permanently gone. I do not miss it. It can be a pretty poor disguise for bad cooking.

I learned to be temperate in my tastes. When I drank alcoholic beverages again, it was one carefully measured drink, and that one infrequently in the beginning. This rule also applied to tea and coffee.

I cannot safely anticipate the advice your doctor will give you as you return to a carefree diet. I think you will be fortunate, however, if your doctor persuades you — as mine did — to:
BE MODERATE, in food and drink.
EAT OFTEN. You should never break this habit if the ulcer diet first made you form it. The big meal at the end of the day after

morning coffee and a hasty, inadequate lunch is certainly less than ideal for anyone.

RETREAT occasionally to your convalescent diet for a few days, especially after immoderate behavior or during times of stress.

WHEN IN DOUBT, do not eat a strange food.

Good health and good appetite.

CHECK LIST OF FOODS

The following check lists are of the foods allowed on most ulcer diets. All, except those starred, are generally allowable in what we have been calling the early phase. The starred foods should not be eaten until the healing process is well along.

Before using these lists, check against those given you by your own doctor. If there is any discrepancy, follow your doctor's lists and change the ones here to conform with his. Or, if you have the opportunity, show these lists to your doctor and ask him to cross off any of the foods here that should not be a part of your particular diet.

List of foods for diet, early and later phases

Apples*
Apricots
Asparagus
Avocados

Bananas
Beans,
  string
  wax
Beef,
  ground lean
  roast
  steaks

Beets, small young
Breads,
  French
  gluten
  melba toast
  rusks
  white
  whole wheat
Broccoli*
Butter

Cakes,
  angel

pound
sponge
Calf's brains
Carrots
Celery
Cherries, white canned
Chicken,
    breast of
    liver
Chocolate*
Coffee substitutes
    Decaf
    Postum
    Sanka
Cookies,
    graham
    sugar
Cottage cheese
Crackers
    plain types
    oysterettes
    saltines
    soda
Cream
Cream cheese

Dried fruits

Eggs

Fish,
    bluefish
    butterfish
    cod
    flounder
    halibut
    mullet
    salmon
    sea bass
    trout
Flour
Fruit nectars

Gelatine

Herbs,*
    basil*
    chervil*
    chives*
    dill weed*
    parsley*
    rosemary*
    sage*
    summer savory*
    tarragon*
Honey

Ice cream

Jellies

Lamb chops,
    loin
    rib
Lemon juice*
Lettuce*
    Bibb*
    Boston*
Liver,
    calf's
    chicken
    lamb

Malted milk
Maple syrup
Margarine
Milk
Mushrooms*

Noodles

Oil,
  olive*
  salad
Orange juice
Oysters*

Pasta,
  macaroni
  pastine
  spaghetti
Peaches
Pears
Peas, green
Potatoes
Prunes

Pudding mixtures

Raisins
Rice, white

Salt
Spinach
Squash,*
  acorn*
  Hubbard*
  zucchini*
Sugars,
  brown
  maple
  white
Sweetbreads

Tapioca
Tomatoes*

Vanilla extract*

Water cress*
Wheat germ

BETWEEN MEALS.

There are few diets which allow for so much between-meal eating as ours. Our rule is to let few hours pass without consuming something. But when one eats between meals on orders, it may prove to be more of a bore than a boon.

As an aside, I admit that I do not approve of the idea that a substitute should pretend to be the food which it replaces. Although I love vegetables, I am not a vegetarian. If I had to exist on vegetables alone, I do not think I would care to eat "vegetable cutlets" and convince myself that they tasted "just like meat."

In the same light, nibbling on dry cereal is not the same as chewing up nutmeats or popcorn. However, they are not unpleasant, unless you happen to loathe them.

Here are a few recipes for healthful, harmless between meal snacks.

Cottage Cheese Variations

This cheese may not be sublime but it can be sublimated. With sweets, it can be classed with desserts, and because of its protein content it can be a main dish or part of a main dish.

No matter how you shudder at the image of Tea Shoppe salads (wilted lettuce, half of a canned peach filled with cottage cheese and an almond — stuffed prune) try cottage cheese with:

> Fruit with its (the fruit's) syrup and cream
> Jellies
> Aspics or gelatins
> Special Mayonnaise (see recipe)
> Cream and
> > honey
> > maple or other sugars
> > puréed fruit

Diced white meat of chicken and diced cooked potatoes with oil or special mayonnaise (our own chef's salad!).

Hot potatoes — preferably baked with butter, cream and a pinch of salt.

These are early phase recipes.

Cream Cheese Variations

The following list is of foods to eat with cream cheese. These can be very tasty on the invariable toast or crackers or the sweeter ones on toasted slices of plain cake.

Jellies
White, brown or maple sugars
Maple syrup
Honey
Minced chicken
Flakes of cooked fish
Bits of cooked beef (leftover steak, roast beef)
Special Mayonnaise (see recipe).

These are early phase recipes.

Dry Cereal Variations

Dry cereal with just sugar and milk can prove tiresome, as can the cereal itself since it has become a staple in our diet. Try some of the following to liven it:

Maple or brown sugar
Jellies
Cottage cheese with milk or cream
Canned fruit with its syrup and milk

These are early phase recipes.

Mashed Avocado

1 very ripe avocado
2 tablespoons oil
2 tablespoons tomato juice
¼ teaspoon salt

2 drops lemon juice
1 hard-cooked egg yolk,
   mashed (optional)

Peel and remove stone from avocado. Mash and blend thoroughly with all other ingredients. Serve on toast or crackers. Will keep for one or two days if covered in refrigerator (although the color may darken). Makes about 1 cup.

This is a later phase recipe. (It is also a very bland variation of Guacamole, of which there are many variations.)

Dry Cereal Snack

Round oats (Cheerios)
or
Rice squares (Rice Chex)

or
Your allowable favorite
Sprinkle of salt

Put a small amount of the cereal in a bowl and sprinkle with a minute amount of salt. Shake the bowl gently and eat the cereal much as you would salted nuts.

This can be a very satisfying snack if you crave something crunchy. Drink your milk with it and the results are the same as eating the cereal in the usual manner. The esthetics of the deed can be quite gratifying.

This is an early phase recipe.

Special Mayonnaise

2 whole eggs
1 cup oil (olive, salad, or what
  you will, including a blend)

½ teaspoon salt
2 to 3 drops lemon juice

Break eggs into the container of the blender (it helps if the eggs are cold), cover and turn switch to high speed. After a few seconds, lift blender cover cautiously and pour oil into the egg very slowly. Egg and oil mixture should emulsify when about half the oil has been added. If it has not, stop adding oil and drop in the lemon juice and salt. Then, continue the oil and blend for 20 seconds after all is added. Mayonnaise should be fairly thick and light yellow in color.

If it has not thickened, pour mixture into a cup and put another whole egg into the blender. Start again, using the egg-oil mixture as you did the first oil, adding it slowly to the new egg.

Store in the refrigerator in a tightly covered glass container. Do not keep or use for longer than a week. Makes about 2 cups mayonnaise.

This is an early phase recipe.

Chopped Chicken Livers
(Ulcer Diet Pâté)

1 pound fresh (or frozen)
   chicken livers
¾ cup water
1 teaspoon salt
   (approximately)

2 hard-cooked eggs
2 tablespoons melted butter (or
   salad oil or Special
   Mayonnaise)

Place chicken livers on steamer rack over boiling water, sprinkle with ½ teaspoon salt and cook for 10 minutes. Discard water and let livers cool. Rub them through a sieve or put through a food mill with the eggs. Blend in the butter (or substitute) and season with the rest of the salt. Pack the livers into a tightly covered jar or crock and keep in the refrigerator. Serve cold on crackers or toast. Makes about 2 cups pâté.

This is an early phase recipe. It is also one you may enjoy for a long time afterwards.

Cold Vegetables

1 or more leftover steamed
potatoes (preferably new or
young ones) or a few cold
cooked carrots

1 tablespoon (or more) oil
⅛ teaspoon salt
1 or 2 drops lemon juice
(later in diet)

Slice or dice vegetables into a small bowl and toss lightly with
oil and salt.

This can be a pleasant dish on a summer "dog" day or that something to eat off toothpicks at a cocktail party. Your alcohol-imbibing friends are certain to be curious and very likely pleased. After
all, many of the more usual tidbits are also in an oil bath. However, the aftertaste of a potato can be far sweeter than a smoked
mussel. (Especially, you may tell them, with gin.)

This is an early phase recipe. (But do not hurry it.)

THE BLENDER

In earlier days, whenever I was asked what I used my blender for, I had to stop and think. I knew that I had wanted one for a long time and that I used it often and not for frozen daiquiris alone. From the beginning of my ulcer diet, I found that I used it daily. Answering the same question brought forth a flood of replies. I have specified blender and food mill in other sections of recipes, these are made entirely in the blender. The malted milk machines of most lunch counters can be used for some of the mixtures. However, they will not purée solid foods.

Basic Blender Meal

1 cup milk	1 tablespoon malted milk
½ cup heavy cream	powder
1 raw egg	1 scoop vanilla ice cream

Place all ingredients in blender container, cover tightly and turn on high speed. Blend for about 30 seconds and turn off machine.

What you are about to drink is a very rich vanilla malted with an egg in it.

From here on and with this general idea, you should be able to go the distance alone. However:

I heard at a lecture on "health foods" that by using certain "constants" in this sort of drink that you could always come up with a pleasant flavor. This is true. Some of the more subtle flavors will always shine through, while others will be masked or completely disappear. You will never taste the raw egg (provided that it is fresh).

This method of "dining" is quick, little trouble and a marvelous way to consume foods that you loathe the taste of, but should eat. Remember always to sip it slowly. Not especially to savor it as you may a vintage wine, but because it is heavy, solid food in a liquid state.

This is an early phase recipe.

Blender Breakfast I

1 cup milk
1 cup cream
½ cup (4 ounces) orange juice
1 egg

½ tablespoon seedless white
  raisins
1 teaspoon instant Sanka

Blend 30 seconds to 1 minute. Sip.

This is an early phase recipe.

Blender Breakfast II

1 cup milk, warm
1 cup cream
½ ripe banana
1 egg

2 tablespoons wheat germ or
  instant-cooking cereal
1 tablespoon honey

Blend 30 seconds to 1 minute. Sip.

This is an early phase recipe.

Blender Breakfast III

1 cup milk
1 cup cream
1 egg
⅜ cup (3 ounces) tomato juice

2 tablespoons wheat germ
1 tablespoon melted butter or
  oil

Blend 30 seconds to 1 minute. Sip.

This is an early phase recipe.

Blender Gazpacho

1 cup half light cream,
 half milk
1 tablespoon olive oil
½ peeled ripe avocado

¼ cup strained tomato pulp or
 ¼ cup tomato juice
¼ teaspoon salt

Blend until smooth. Sip or eat from a bowl, having poured gazpacho over broken pieces of toast.

This is is a later phase recipe.

Blended With Fruit I

1 cup half light cream,
 half milk
1 ripe peach, peeled and pitted

1 tablespoon honey
2 to 3 tablespoons pineapple
 sherbet

Blend until smooth. Serve with thin sugar cookies.

This is is a later phase recipe.

Blended With Fruit II

1 cup half light cream,
 half milk
Small can peeled pears
 (use entire contents)

1 scoop vanilla ice cream
1 tablespoon chocolate syrup
 (optional, or use maple sugar)

Blend until smooth. Sip.

This is an early phase recipe.

You can make a melange of neutral taste or you can capitalize on a single flavor. If you do not like the taste of a particular brew, do not junk it. Put it back into the blender and add something you do like or something with an indestructible flavor, for example, a banana.

This list of ingredients from which to choose I think, covers about all the ground, but I may have missed something, so please feel free to add to it.

milk
cream
eggs
ice cream
sherbet
oil or melted butter
malted milk powder
chocolate syrup
maple syrup
honey
any or all sugars
seedless white raisins
fresh pears, peaches, bananas

applesauce
canned fruits
nectars and juices
custard
avocados
cooked vegetables
vegetable juices
wheat germ
instant-cooking cereals
dry cereals
instant Sanka, Postum or
  other caffeinless coffee

Blender Sandwich Spreads

The puréed nature of these foods makes almost all of them applicable for the early phase of the diet. However a little caution should be applied. The foods should be placed in the blender in the order given in the recipe. Never let the motor run if the blender binds; shut it off immediately and stir the food with a rubber spatula. If the mixture is too thick add a little liquid, salad oil or milk and resume blending.

The ingredients listed make from 1 to 2 cups of sandwich spread. These will keep for a day or two in covered glass jars in the refrigerator.

I

3 ounce package cream cheese
½ cup diced cooked white
  meat of chicken

1 egg
¼ cup salad oil

II

1 cup diced lean roast beef
½ cup diced cooked potato
1 egg

¼ cup salad oil
⅛ teaspoon salt

III

1 cup flaked cooked fish
¼ cup diced cooked carrot
1 egg

¼ cup salad oil
2 to 3 drops lemon juice

IV

½ cup diced cooked white
  meat of chicken
3 broiled chicken livers
3 steamed mushroom caps

1 egg
¼ cup salad oil
⅛ teaspoon salt

V

3 hard-cooked eggs, sliced   ¼ cup salad oil
½ cup cottage cheese   ⅛ teaspoon salt
1 raw egg

These are later phase recipes.

EGGS

The best foods are the most versatile.

A steak is a steak is a steak; but an egg can be anything. Boiled, poached, coddled, scrambled, or lost in the flavors of other foods, an egg is the pearl of the kitchen. My enthusiasm may be running away with my thoughts, but after water and salt, I think there is no other thing we reach for as often in cooking almost any cuisine.

From the mayonnaise on our hors d'oeuvre to the custard of our dessert we are aided and abetted by the egg. These may be the garnishings of a meal, for to some the way of the omelet is supreme. Or the soufflé or the cold hard-cooked, salt-sprinkled egg eaten out of its shell while you are standing up somewhere (in the partly constructed, wind blown frame of a dream house).

To M. F. K. Fisher, I send an especially fine and fresh dozen of these pearls. The "Unfried Eggs" are her creation. I am grateful for these and for many pleasurable hours of reading and for sustaining thoughts of eating.

Unfried Eggs

1 to 2 tablespoons butter   2 eggs

Melt butter in a heavy skillet that has been well heated. Gently break eggs into the butter and immediately remove the pan from the heat. Cover the skillet and wait 3 minutes.

The results are (to my taste) a good bit heartier than a coddled egg and easier than a baked one. Makes 1 serving.

This is an early phase recipe. It can be felicitously soothing at any time and for anyone.

Hard-Cooked Eggs

Eggs are never boiled, they are cooked.

Cook eggs in simmering water 15 to 20 minutes. Cool them immediately in cold water.

They are ready to eat in their natural shape, or you can slice them, chop them, or mash them fine.

Egg paste made with either mayonnaise or softened butter and perhaps a bit of avocado or vegetable purée is a fine way to use them in mashed form. It is useful on crackers, toast, or as a sandwich filling.

This is an early phase recipe.

Egg à la Russe

1 hard-cooked egg
2 tablespoons Special
  Mayonnaise (see recipe)
1 tablespoon tomato juice

Small piece of ripe avocado
  (optional)
1 drop lemon juice

Cut egg into quarters. Mix, mash and blend other ingredients and arrange a blob of the sauce over each egg quarter. Makes 1 serving.

This is a later phase recipe.

Soft-Cooked Eggs and Coddled Eggs

There are two methods for soft-cooking eggs. You can lower them into simmering water, if the eggs are at room temperature. Or you can put them cold into cold water and heat the water slowly to the simmering point.

A coddled egg, properly speaking, is not cooked at all. It is placed in a pot of boiling water and covered. The pot is then removed from the source of heat. Time carefully for 8 minutes, longer if a firmer yolk is desired. Remove and serve.

This is an early phase recipe.

Scrambled Eggs

Eggs   A little milk or water
Butter

Beat eggs and milk or water only enough to blend the white, the
yolk, and the liquid. Heat a heavy skillet over a very low flame
and melt butter in it. Pour in the beaten eggs and let them begin
to set. Lift the coagulated egg with a fork as it cooks until all of
it is firm and moist. Remove the pan from the heat, scramble
and serve.

Another method (far slower) is to do the same thing using the
upper pan of a double boiler instead of the skillet. The lower
pan is to be kept full of boiling water.

A third way is to use the chafing dish. For this be extra lavish
with the sweet butter and at the last minute add a spoonful or
two of good sweet jelly.

This is an early phase recipe.

Shirred Eggs

Eggs   Toast or bread crumbs
Butter

Use little, shallow baking dishes (ramekins) which should be
heated and buttered. Start the oven at moderate, 350° F. Place
the buttered dishes in a shallow pan containing a little hot water.
Or use 325° F. and omit the pan and water both. Add buttered
toast or bread crumbs to each dish. Break the eggs carefully over
the toast or crumbs. Put another dot of butter on each egg yolk,
place the pan in the oven, and bake until firm, about 15 minutes.
Remove dishes from pan, wipe off, and serve at once. Each dish
makes 1 serving.

This is an early phase recipe.

Poached Eggs

Eggs   Salt
Water

Bring salted water to a gentle boil. Carefully break eggs into the water (or into an egg poacher) and poach for about 3 minutes, or until the whites are set. The water should not boil again after the eggs have been added to it. Remove the eggs with a perforated spoon.

Serve on toast.

Serve floating on creamed soup.

Serve on a bed of lavishly buttered mashed potatoes.

Serve Poached Eggs (almost) Florentine: Make a bed of puréed spinach, top with poached eggs and a dollop of Special Mayonnaise. This is equally effective on any puréed vegetable or on cottage cheese.

This is an early phase recipe.

OMELETS

Basic Omelet

2 eggs
⅛ teaspoon salt

2 tablespoons water, milk or
cream (optional)
1 tablespoon butter

Beat eggs, salt, and liquid thoroughly. Heat a heavy small pan over a high flame and add the butter. When the butter is hot, lower the heat and pour in the eggs. Lift the cooked mass of the eggs and let the liquid part run underneath until all the liquid is gone. Fold and serve at once on a heated plate. Makes 1 serving.

This is an early phase recipe.

Omelet Soufflé

4 eggs
⅛ teaspoon salt

3 tablespoons butter

Separate the eggs. Beat the whites until stiff and season with the salt. Beat the yolks until lemon colored and fold into the whites. Blend thoroughly and pour into buttered pan. Cook over low heat and finish in a moderately slow oven or bake the omelet completely in a moderately slow oven, 300 to 325° F. Serve at once.

Makes 1 or 2 servings.

This is an early phase recipe.

Omelet Soufflé Variations

You can add to the basic mixture or top the finished omelet with cooked foods and fold it. They are particularly good as desserts with jelly or stewed fruit, but they also are delicious with vegetables.

To add to the basic mixture, beat any of the following into the yolks (after they have been beaten until lemon colored and thick.)

3 tablespoons puréed spinach
   or carrots or broccoli
or
3 tablespoons applesauce,
   puréed apricots, or peaches

2 tablespoons sugar
or
2 tablespoons crabapple jelly
   or another of your choice

These are early phase recipes.

Oyster Omelet

Basic Omelet (see recipe)
6 oysters
2 tablespoons butter

½ tablespoon flour
½ cup heavy cream
¼ teaspoon salt

Shuck oysters, reserve their liquid and chop them coarsely. Melt butter in a small saucepan, add flour and stir until well blended. Add oysters, their juice, cream and salt. Cook over low heat, stirring constantly, until sauce is thick and oyster pieces start to curl.

Prepare basic omelet. Pour creamed oysters over it, fold and serve. Makes 2 servings.

This is a later phase recipe.

Sole Omelet

Basic Omelet (see recipe)   ½ cup Cream Sauce
½ cup flaked cooked sole   (see recipe)

Combine and heat Cream Sauce and sole. Make basic omelet.
Pour creamed sole over it, fold and serve.

This is an early phase recipe.

Chicken Liver Omelet

Basic Omelet (see recipe)   2 tablespoons herb butter
2 chicken livers   (chive, tarragon or parsley)
1 tablespoon butter   ¼ teaspoon salt

Broil the chicken livers, basting them with 1 tablespoon butter.
When they are done, chop them coarsely. Melt the herb butter,
season with salt and add the livers.

Make a basic omelet. Pour the chicken livers and sauce over it,
fold and serve. Makes 1 serving.

This is a later phase recipe.

Salmon Omelet

Basic Omelet (see recipe)   ½ cup flaked cooked salmon
2 tablespoons Herb Butter
  (dill flavored) (see recipe)

Melt herb butter and add flaked salmon. Heat to warm the fish
but do not cook it further. Make basic omelet, add fish, fold and
serve. Makes 1 or 2 servings.

This is a later phase recipe.

Banana Omelet

Basic Omelet (see recipe)
1 ripe banana

1 tablespoon (or more to taste) brown or maple sugar

Make a basic omelet. Drop sliced banana (or sliced peach, or canned fruit) over it. Sprinkle with the sugar. Fold and serve. Makes 1 serving.

This is an early phase recipe.

Apple Omelet

Basic Omelet (see recipe)
1 large or 2 small cored baked apples

1 tablespoon butter
1 tablespoon brown sugar

Remove all skin from apples. Dice and add to melted butter, add sugar. Heat but do not cook.

Make basic omelet and add apples, fold and serve. Makes 1 serving.

This is a later phase recipe.

Deviled Eggs

2 hard-cooked eggs
2 tablespoons Special Mayonnaise (see recipe)

1 tablespoon softened herb butter (chive)

Slice eggs in half lengthwise. Remove yolks carefully and mash with mayonnaise and butter. Fill egg whites with yolk mixture.

This is a later phase recipe.

Eggs Aurore

2 poached eggs
2 slices trimmed toast,
   buttered

2 tablespoons Special
   Mayonnaise (see recipe)
1 tablespoon toasted bread
   crumbs

Arrange toast in shallow heated baking dish and top with poached eggs. Drop a tablespoon of mayonnaise on each egg yolk and sprinkle with bread crumbs. Place under broiler for 1 minute and serve immediately.

This is a later phase recipe.

Eggs Florentine

2 poached eggs
2 slices trimmed toast,
   buttered

¼ cup creamed spinach
   (can be baby food)
2 tablespoons Special
   Mayonnaise (see recipe)

Arrange toast on heated baking dish and top with poached eggs. Cover the egg white with a ring of creamed spinach, top the yolk with 1 tablespoon mayonnaise. Place under broiler for 1 minute and serve immediately.

This is a later phase recipe.

Eggs and Mushrooms

2 eggs, lightly beaten with
1 tablespoon light cream
1 tablespoon butter

4 mushroom caps, steamed
  and chopped
⅛ teaspoon salt

Melt the butter in top of double boiler over boiling water. Add eggs, mushrooms, and salt. Cook until set, stirring to form curds.

This is a later phase recipe.

Eggs in Cream

2 eggs

¼ cup light cream

Heat cream in a small baking dish or ramekin. Break eggs into the cream and bake in a moderate, 350° F., oven until set.

This is an early phase recipe.

Eggs Marinière

2 eggs
1 tablespoon butter
4 oysters, chopped

2 tablespoons light cream
2 tablespoons young spinach,
  chopped

Melt butter in small baking dish, add oysters, cream, and spinach and break eggs carefully into the mixture. Bake in a moderate, 350° F., oven until eggs are set.

This is a later phase recipe.

Mirror Eggs

2 eggs   Butter

Lightly butter a flat baking dish and break 2 new fresh eggs into it. Place in a hot, 450° F., oven or under broiler for 1 minute. The milky film on the egg whites will seem to reflect images.

This is a variation on coddled eggs.

This is an early phase recipe.

Eggs Niçoise

2 cold poached eggs   ¼ cup early peas
Soft leaves of Boston or Bibb   3 tablespoons Special
    lettuce   Mayonnaise (see recipe)
¼ cup diced cold cooked potato

Arrange lettuce to form a nest and place eggs into it. Sprinkle potato and peas over eggs and top with mayonnaise.

This is a later phase recipe.

Eggs à la Reine

2 poached eggs
2 pieces of toast,
  trimmed

¼ cup cooked white meat
  of chicken
¼ cup Special Mayonnaise
  (see recipe)

Make the chicken and most of the mayonnaise into a purée. This can be done in the blender or by pounding with mortar and pestle. Spread the purée on the toast and top with the eggs and the rest of the mayonnaise. Broil for 1 minute under medium broiler flame. Can also be served cold.

This is a later phase recipe.

SOUP

It is a rare household in which the soup kettle has a place of honor or even use. The infinite range of canned, frozen, and packaged soup mixes has proven to be the most satisfactory of our prepared foods. But we are cut off from this supply for almost all of them contain forbidden fruit or are cooked in ways for other palates than ours.

Soup and a piece of bread has long been known to satisfy the peasant's hunger. It can be the complete meal, and I have often found that it can be one of the most soothing meals.

Our soups exclude what is essential in all good French (or other) cookbooks: the meat stock. The electric blender, the careful preparation of the ingredients, our good cream and butter all contribute mightily towards making up for this lack. They may be "soupless" soups but they are exceedingly good.

Beet Juice Borscht

1 bunch small young beets   ½ teaspoon salt
1 quart water   1 teaspoon lemon juice
2 tablespoons sugar

Wash and scrub beets, peel and grate. Put in a 1½ quart kettle with all other ingredients and cook at a low boil or simmer 45 minutes. Let cool, and strain the juice. Makes 4 to 6 servings. Will keep well under refrigeration for 2 or 3 days.

To serve:
Put a large spoonful of lightly salted whipped cream into each serving.

Or beat one egg until frothy for each serving and blend with the borscht.

This is a later phase recipe.

Cherry Soup

½ pound dry Bing cherries   1 tablespoon brown sugar
   (or prunes or apricots)   1 teaspoon lemon juice
   1 cup water   1 cup light cream

Soak fruit in the 1 cup cold water for 4 hours (or overnight), add lemon juice and sugar and simmer 20 minutes. Let cool, then chill fruit and add cream, blending thoroughly. Fruit may be pitted before cooking or cooked fruit may be forced through food mill. To serve warm, heat very carefully. Garnish with whipped cream. Makes 3 or 4 servings.

This is a later phase recipe.

Cream of Avocado Soup

1 ripe avocado
1 tablespoon oil
1 cup milk

⅛ teaspoon salt
1 drop green pure food
  coloring

Peel and slice avocado. Place avocado and all other ingredients in blender and blend until smooth. Serve with tiny squares of buttered toast floating on the surface of the soup. Serve chilled or heat very carefully. Makes 2 small servings.

This is an early phase recipe.

Cream of Celery Soup

1 stalk celery
½ cup water
¼ teaspoon salt
3 tablespoons butter

1½ tablespoons flour
1 cup milk
½ cup light cream

Wash and trim celery. Cut (leaves and all) into slices across the entire stalk and boil in salted water 20 minutes. Put celery and cooking liquid through food mill. Melt butter and cook with flour for 1 minute. Heat milk and cream and add to butter and flour, cook, stirring constantly until it begins to thicken. Add the celery purée and continue cooking over low heat for 5 minutes. Makes 2 small servings.

This is an early phase recipe.

Fresh Bean Soup

½ pound of string or wax
   beans (fresh or frozen)
½ cup water
1 medium potato, peeled
  and diced

¼ teaspoon salt
1 cup milk
2 tablespoons butter

Wash and string fresh beans or defrost frozen beans. Place water, potato, and salt in pan, place steamer over the potato and fill with beans (or sliced zucchini). Cover tightly. Boil and steam 12 minutes. Force all vegetables and liquid through food mill. Heat milk and butter, add purée and simmer 3 minutes over low heat. Do not boil. Serve hot. Makes 2 servings.

This is an early phase recipe.

Cream of Water Cress Soup

¼ pound water cress (about 1
   cup chopped and pressed
   down) (or young spinach
   or Boston lettuce)

¾ cup water
¼ teaspoon salt
1 cup light cream
3 tablespoons butter

Cut away any tough stems on water cress or other vegetables, cook in salted water 5 or 6 minutes. Put through food mill with cooking liquid. Heat cream and butter and add vegetable purée. Simmer 3 minutes over low heat. Serve hot or chilled. Garnish with chopped hard-cooked egg. Makes 2 servings.

This is a later phase recipe.

Potato Soup

2 medium potatoes, peeled
  and diced fine
2 tablespoons small square
  noodles

3 tablespoons butter
½ teaspoon salt
1 cup water

Combine all ingredients in covered pan and simmer gently 30 minutes, or until potatoes and noodles are almost dissolved. Add a little water or milk if too thick. Garnish with diced cooked white meat of chicken or crumbled leftover broiled chopped steak. Makes 2 servings.

This is a later phase recipe.

Cream of Carrot Soup

1 bunch small young carrots
½ cup water
¼ teaspoon salt

1 cup milk
2 tablespoons butter

Wash and scrape carrots and cut into small pieces. Cook in salted water until soft. Mash carrots in the cooking liquid until smooth (or put through blender). Heat milk and butter and add carrots. Simmer over low heat 3 minutes. Serve hot or cold garnished with lightly salted whipped cream. Makes 2 servings.

This is an early phase recipe.

Cream of Asparagus Soup

Tips of 1 pound asparagus
½ cup water
⅛ teaspoon salt

1 cup milk
2 tablespoons butter

Wash asparagus carefully, drain. Steam over salted water 10 minutes. Force asparagus and water through food mill. Heat milk and butter and add asparagus purée. Simmer 3 minutes, serve hot or chilled. May be garnished with lightly salted whipped cream. Makes 2 servings.

This is an early phase recipe.

Cream of Mushroom Soup

Caps from ½ pound
   mushrooms
½ cup water
⅛ teaspoon salt

1 cup light cream or milk
2 tablespoons butter
1 teaspoon chives
   (optional)

Place steamer in pan over boiling water. Place mushroom caps on steamer with stem side down. Sprinkle with salt and add chives. Cover tightly and steam 15 minutes. Discard chives and cooking liquid. Reduce the mushroom caps to a purée in the blender, add a little light cream or milk if mixture is too thick to blend. Heat remaining cream and butter and add purée. Simmer 5 minutes over low heat. Makes 2 servings.

This is a later phase recipe.

Cream of Pea Soup

1 package (8 to 10 oz.) frozen
    early peas
½ cup water

⅛ teaspoon salt
1 cup light cream
2 tablespoons butter

Steam the peas over salted water for 4 minutes. Add water and peas to blender and blend at high speed until smooth. Heat the cream and butter and add pea purée. Simmer for 3 minutes and serve hot or chilled. Makes 2 servings.

This is an early phase recipe.

Oyster Stew

1 dozen oysters
1 cup light cream
1 cup milk

⅛ teaspoon salt
2 tablespoons butter

Defrost frozen oysters; look over fresh bulk oysters for bits of shell. Cook oysters over low heat in their own liquid until the edges curl. Heat milk and cream to boiling point and add to oysters. Add salt and butter and serve immediately. Makes 2 servings.

This is a later phase recipe.

Apple Soup

2 large apples, cored and baked
2 large apples, peeled and
  cored
1 medium potato, peeled and
  quartered
3 tablespoons water

¼ teaspoon salt
  2 tablespoons brown sugar
  1 cup milk
½ cup light cream
  3 tablespoons butter

Bake 2 apples and reserve them. Put 2 peeled apples and the potato through the blender. Cook the purée with 3 tablespoons of water, salt, and brown sugar over low heat in a covered pan for 15 minutes, add a little more water from time to time, if necessary. Heat milk, cream, and butter and slowly add to cooked purée. Continue cooking over low heat, stirring 5 minutes. Peel and dice the baked apples and roll in a little brown sugar. Use this as a garnish for the soup. May be served hot or chilled. Makes 2 servings.

This is a later phase recipe.

Vegetable Consommé, Hot

I have mentioned elsewhere that it is a good idea to save the vegetable juices from cooked, steamed, and canned vegetables. These may be added to tomato juice; and simply served mixed for a satisfying soup, alone in a cup or garnished with rice, noodles or Cottage Cheese Dumplings (see recipe). Later in the diet we may add a drop of lemon juice or steep a sprig of herb in the soup.

We can boil vegetables (mixed) in large quantities of water for the broth, discarding the vegetables, and we can use some of the water in which rice, pasta, or dried beans have been cooked. (Julius Caesar drank quantities of barley water for the ulcers he was supposed to have had.)

This is an early phase recipe.

Vegetable Consommé, Jellied

The same vegetable juices that we drink hot or cold may have gelatin added to them. They make a fine substitute for the sometimes rather pallid madrilène, especially the canned variety.

1½ cups vegetable juice   2 tablespoons cold water
  1 envelope gelatin

Soften the gelatin in cold water. Heat vegetable juice and add gelatin. Let cool and then chill until set. Serve with lightly salted whipped cream. Makes 2 small servings.

This is an early phase recipe.

Variation:

Make 2 kinds, mixed vegetable juice, and all tomato. Keep each separate until serving time. Toss the jellied consommé lightly in the serving cups. The colors and flavors are very good together.

Soup Garnishes

The little extra touch can make soup a main dish.

Rice and any form of noodles are expected.

Cut-up pieces of broiled chicken liver, chopped steak, diced cooked chicken, buttered toast tidbits (not quite croûtons) and light dumplings all help extend the heartiness of soup.

Chicken Quenelle Garnish

2 chicken breasts, boned
  and skinned
2 eggs

½ teaspoon salt
2 cups light cream

Grind the chicken breasts very fine. Put the meat, eggs and salt in the blender and blend until smooth. Gradually add the cream. Chill the mixture, form it into small balls and poach in salted water that is simmering, not boiling. Makes enough to garnish 4 soup plates.

This is a later phase recipe.

Cold Potato Soup

Vichyssoise is not the only cold creamed soup, the average restaurateur may be shocked to learn. The technique for cooking it may be adapted for vegetables other than leeks.

This is a general recipe, most any of the vegetables may be used (see list).

2 medium potatoes, peeled and diced	¾ cup water
	¼ teaspoon salt
1 cup chopped vegetable	3 tablespoons butter
(zucchini, string beans, etc.)	1 cup light cream

Cook or steam vegetables in salted water until tender. Add butter and purée, using all liquid from cooking. Do not use blender for vegetables with fiber (string beans, asparagus, and so on). Allow purée to cool. Then chill and mix thoroughly with cold cream and serve. Makes 2 servings.

This is an early phase recipe. Later we may season the soups with herb butters.

Cream of Vegetable Soup

The flavors from the many vegetables and their cooking liquid combine to make a soup very similar to that cooked with marrow bones and meat. The vegetables listed serve as a guide, substitutions according to taste and season may be made. Using the food mill rather than the blender will eliminate the fibrous matter and make it possible to use food otherwise proscribed. This soup will keep under refrigeration or it may be frozen. The recipe makes a large quantity.

1 quart water	6 small carrots, scraped and
1 tablespoon salt	quartered
2 tablespoons sugar	1 ear of fresh corn
4 medium potatoes, peeled	1 cup shelled baby lima beans
and quartered	1 cup wax or string beans
2 to 3 large beefsteak tomatoes	1 turnip or 2 zucchini
2 stalks celery with leaves	Small bunch of parsley or
	water cress

Bring the water, salt and sugar to a boil in a large tightly covered kettle. Add all other ingredients, cover, bring to a boil, reduce heat and simmer 15 minutes. Let the vegetables cool, force through the food mill (if you use the blender, the purée will have to be strained through a fine sieve). Scrape the kernels off the ear of corn into the food mill with the other vegetables. Replace the purée in the kettle and stir it thoroughly, cook over low heat for 20 minutes. It is now ready to serve or store in the refrigerator.

To serve:

1 cup vegetable purée	1 to 2 tablespoons butter
½ cup milk or light cream	

Heat all ingredients together and simmer 2 to 3 minutes. Makes 1 large serving.

This is a later phase recipe.

Cream of Tomato Soup

¾ cup milk
⅛ teaspoon salt
 1 tablespoon butter

1 cup hot Tomato Bouillon
 (see recipe)

Heat the milk, salt and butter, add the hot bouillon slowly. Stir to prevent curdling. May be garnished with a little cooked rice. Makes 2 small servings.

This is a later phase recipe.

Tomato Bouillon

1 pound fresh ripe tomatoes,
 quartered
¼ cup water

¼ teaspoon salt
2 to 3 drops lemon juice
1 tablespoon sugar

Combine all ingredients in a heavy kettle, cover and cook at a boil 15 minutes. Let cool. Force all pulp and juice through a food mill. Reheat juice over low heat for 5 minutes. Serve hot or cold. Makes 2 servings.

This is a later phase recipe.

Large beefsteak tomatoes are the best variety to use. The juice will freeze well and may be made in late summer for winter use. If canned tomatoes are used, choose a good variety and use ½ the quantity of water.

Variations:
Add 2 tablespoons of uncooked rice or pastine and 2 tablespoons of butter to the bouillon and cook until tender.

Cream of Broccoli Soup

1 pound fresh broccoli
1 cup water
⅛ teaspoon salt

1 cup milk
1 tablespoon butter

Wash broccoli, look over carefully, and trim the thick stem sections away. Sprinkle with salt. Steam over boiling water 8 minutes. Force through food mill. Heat milk and butter, add purée and cook over low heat 5 minutes, stirring often. May be garnished with diced white cooked meat of chicken or tiny meat balls made of broiled lean beef. Makes 2 servings.

This is an early phase recipe.

Fish Bisque

1 medium potato, peeled
  and diced
1 cup water
¼ teaspoon salt
1 pound fillet of sole

1 teaspoon lemon juice
1 cup milk
1 cup light cream
2 tablespoons butter
¼ teaspoon salt

Boil potato in the cup of water with the first ¼ teaspoon of salt for 5 minutes. Add sole and lemon juice, cook 10 minutes longer or until fish flakes to the touch of a fork. Drain the fish and potato and mash them very fine. Heat the milk, cream, butter and second salt, add the fish and blend thoroughly, cook 3 minutes over very low heat. Add a few drops of red pure food coloring, if desired. The soup can be served with rice or Cottage Cheese Dumplings (see recipe). Makes 4 small servings.

This is a later phase recipe.

Minestrone

¼ cup macaroni
½ teaspoon salt
1 quart boiling water
½ cup diced carrots
½ cup diced potato
½ cup chopped tender spinach

½ cup shredded Boston lettuce
   (optional)
½ cup Tomato Purée
   (see recipe)
3 tablespoons olive oil
½ cup cottage cheese

Cook macaroni and salt in boiling water until soft. Add carrots and potato and cook for 5 minutes, then add spinach, lettuce, tomato purée, and olive oil. Cook in an open or loosely covered soup pot for 30 minutes. Macaroni and vegetables should be very limp, almost dissolved. Stir in the cottage cheese and cook for 5 more minutes. Makes 4 servings.

This is a later phase recipe.

Japanese Consommé

2½ cups vegetable juice
   2 small carrots, scraped
   2 tiny new potatoes,
      scrubbed

2 tablespoons diced white meat
   of chicken
2 to 3 drops lemon juice
2 small sprigs parsley

Cut the carrots into decorative shape and cook them and the whole potatoes in the vegetable juice. Add the diced chicken and lemon juice and serve with a tiny sprig of parsley in each bowl. Makes 2 servings.

This is a later phase recipe.

Green Pea Consommé

1 pound shelled early peas or   2 to 3 sprigs water cress
   1 package frozen early peas   ½ cup heavy cream
¼ teaspoon salt   ⅛ teaspoon salt

Cook peas in water with ¼ teaspoon salt for 5 to 6 minutes. Run peas, water, and water cress through blender at high speed. Reheat soup for 1 to 2 minutes. Whip cream until stiff and add salt. Serve soup with generous scoop of whipped cream floating on top. Makes 2 to 3 servings.

This is a later phase recipe.

FISH

Beefsteak is supposed to be the leader of the foods most frequently ordered in restaurants. I would venture to say that lobster, tails or entire, is the usual "fish" order.

People are often "allergic" to fish and shellfish. Perhaps the first times these foods were served to them the preparation was so poor that a hard shell of prejudice was formed.

We do not seem to take enough interest in the variety of fish available in our own locale or those to be had in most markets. So often what we eat or cook as fish is anonymous, a kind of sole. But the fillets are cut from a fish we do not identify.

There are three rules for serving seafood: freshness, quick cooking, and simplicity of seasoning. A fresh fish or fresh shellfish should be cooked carefully and only long enough for it to become just done, and then served in the honorable state of its own flavor.

Poached Fish

Poaching or steaming fish with very little water and as quickly as possible results in tasty, versatile eating. The fish is good hot or cold, plain or combined with other foods.

Sole, salmon, cod, or halibut are good fish for poaching.

1 to 2 pounds fish, cleaned ready to cook; or fillets	½ teaspoon salt
1 cup water	2 to 3 drops lemon juice

Place fish on rack or into water with salt and lemon juice. Cover and steam or cook 12 to 15 minutes. Remove from water immediately. Fish should be firm but flake easily if tested with a fork. Count ¼ to ½ pound as 1 serving.

This is an early phase recipe.

For later phase add a sprig of herb to the water.

Cold Fish

Leftover cold poached fish may be used as a seafood "cocktail." Toss each half cup of flaked fish with 2 tablespoons of Special Mayonnaise (see recipe). Makes 1 serving.

Fish salads may be made combining the flaked fish, mayonnaise and diced cooked potatoes, carrots or ripe avocado.

Fish Pie

1½ cups flaked cooked fish
1 cup Cream Sauce
  (see recipe)
½ cup sliced cooked carrots
2 tablespoons Herb Butter,
  dill flavored (see recipe)

2 medium potatoes, diced
  and cooked
2 tablespoons butter
1 egg
¼ teaspoon salt

Mix and heat, fish, Cream Sauce, carrots and dill butter. Mash potatoes with butter, egg and salt. Line a pie pan with the potatoes to form a bottom "crust". Spoon the fish mixture into the pie. Bake in a moderate, 350° F., oven for 15 minutes. Makes 3 or 4 servings.

This is a later phase recipe.

Creamed Fish and Vegetables

1 cup flaked cooked fish
1 cup thin Cream Sauce
  (see recipe)
1 large potato, diced and
  cooked

2 small carrots, sliced and
  cooked
¼ cup cooked early peas
  (later phase only)

Combine all ingredients and heat over low flames. Makes 2 servings.

This is an early phase recipe.

Broiled Fish

Sole, salmon, halibut, trout, bluefish, flounder and butterfish are good fish for broiling. Avoid very oily fish. Do not eat fish skin.

Oil the pan or broiling rack very lightly so that the fish will not stick to it. Dust fish fillets with flour. Broil fish under low broiler heat about 10 minutes on each side. Dot with butter just before the fish is done. To avoid dry fish, watch the fish rather than the time until you judge it to be done. Count ¼ to ½ pound as 1 serving.

This is a later phase recipe.

Cod in Egg Sauce

1 pound fresh cod, cleaned   ½ teaspoon salt
   and skinned   1 egg
1 cup milk

Place cod, milk and salt in a saucepan, cover and cook over low heat 12 minutes, or until the fish flakes if tested with a fork. Remove the fish to a warmed platter and keep warm. Beat the egg until lemon colored and add it slowly to the hot milk. Continue cooking over low heat, stirring constantly until the mixture thickens. Pour the sauce over the fish and serve with steamed rice. Makes 2 servings.

This is an early phase recipe.

Poached Fish Balls

2 pounds fillets whitefish fillets
2 eggs
2 tablespoons cracker crumbs
½ teaspoon salt
1 tablespoon sugar
1 tablespoon cold water

2 quarts boiling water
1 teaspoon salt
1 teaspoon lemon juice
6 medium carrots, scraped
   and sliced

Grind fish fillets very fine. Place ground fish in a heavy bowl and mash with a potato masher, add eggs 1 at a time and work into a paste. Add cracker crumbs, ½ teaspoon salt, the sugar and cold water and continue mashing until mixture is well blended and smooth.

Keep water at a rolling boil and add 1 teaspoon each of lemon juice and salt. Add sliced carrots and cook 4 minutes. Drop fish paste into the boiling water a teaspoonful at a time, never letting the boiling stop. When all the fish balls are in the water, reduce heat, cover saucepan and cook at a very low boil for 45 minutes. Serve hot or chilled. Makes 4 servings.

This is a later phase recipe.

Salmon Soufflé

3 tablespoons butter
2 tablespoons flour
1 cup light cream
½ teaspoon salt

3 egg yolks, well beaten
1 cup flaked cooked salmon
4 stiffly beaten egg whites
Bread crumbs

Melt butter and cook flour in it for 1 minute, add cream and cook until thick, season with salt. Let cool slightly and beat in egg yolks. Fold in salmon and egg whites. Butter 1 quart soufflé dish and pour in mixture. Top with a sprinkling of bread crumbs. Set dish in shallow pan of hot water and bake in moderate, 350° F., oven for 35 minutes. Serve immediately. Makes 2 to 4 servings.

This is a later phase recipe.

Salmon en Gelée

½ pound salmon steak
½ cup water
1 cup vegetable juice
¼ cup cooked diced carrots

¼ cup cooked early peas
1 envelope gelatin
2 tablespoons cold water
2 to 3 drops lemon juice

Poach salmon in ½ cup water for 15 minutes. Discard water and allow salmon to cool. Heat vegetable juice and add gelatin that has been softened in cold water. Add vegetables and lemon juice. Allow gelatin to cool, and pour a little into a shallow mold, place salmon in the mold, and pour the remaining gelatin over it. Chill in the refrigerator till firm, unmold, and serve garnished with Special Mayonnaise.

This is a later phase recipe.

Poached Sea Bass

3 to 4 pound sea bass
2 cups water
1 thin slice lemon
¼ teaspoon salt
6 hard-cooked eggs

1 egg
⅛ teaspoon salt
2 to 3 drops lemon juice
4 to 6 young spinach leaves
1 sprig parsley

Bring the water to a boil with salt and lemon slice. Poach the fish in simmering water 40 to 45 minutes. Place it on a platter and serve hot or cold with the following garnish sauce:

Put the raw egg in the blender and turn on high speed. Add the oil slowly to make mayonnaise. Season with the salt, lemon juice, and add the spinach and parsley. Cut the 6 hard-cooked eggs in half lengthwise and remove the yolks. Add the yolks to the mayonnaise, and blend ½ minute. Heat the egg whites with the green sauce and arrange them around the fish. Any remaining sauce may be served in a sauce boat. Makes 4 servings.

This is a later phase recipe.

Baked Flounder

2 1-pound flounders, cleaned
   and split
1 cup water
2 thin slices lemon
¼ teaspoon salt

½ teaspoon cut chives
1 carrot, sliced thinly
1 medium potato, sliced
   thinly
3 tablespoons butter

Pour water into shallow baking dish and add lemon, salt, chives, carrot, and potato. Lay fish with skin side up in pan and dot with butter. Bake in moderate, 375° F., oven for 30 minutes or until fish tests done. Dieter should not eat vegetables or pan juices. Makes 4 servings.

This is a later phase recipe.

Sole Bonne Femme

1 pound sole fillets	3 tablespoons butter
6 steamed mushroom caps	2 to 3 tablespoons milk
½ cup cooked spinach	1 cup Cream Sauce
2 medium potatoes, boiled	(see recipe)

Make a purée of the mushrooms, spinach, potatoes, and 2 table-spoons of the butter. Thin with milk, if needed. This may be done in the blender. Spread a layer of the purée in the bottom of a baking dish and arrange the fish fillets over it. Dot the fish with the remaining butter and bake in a moderate, 375° F., oven for 15 minutes or until he fish tests done. Pour the hot cream sauce over it and place under the broiler flame for 1 to 2 minutes. Makes 2 servings.

This is a later phase recipe.

Grilled Mullet

Mullet, cleaned
Parsley
Dill weed or tarragon

Melted butter
Boiled new potatoes

Heat broiler grill (or use charcoal grill) and place fish on top of a liberal nest of the herbs. Cook slowly over low heat (or maximum distance from coals). Turn fish carefully so as not to break the skin. Serve with melted butter and boiled new potatoes.

This is a later phase recipe.

Poached Trout

2 fresh trout
2 cups water
1 sliced carrot
1 thin lemon slice

2 sprigs parsley
¼ teaspoon salt
½ teaspoon cut chives
Melted butter

Boil water and add all ingredients except the trout, cook 3 minutes and add the fish. Cook slightly above the simmer point 12 to 15 minutes. Remove the fish carefully so as not to break them and serve them with melted butter. Makes 2 servings.

This is a later phase recipe.

Baked Stuffed Bluefish

3 to 3½ pound bluefish, split,
cleaned and boned
2 medium potatoes
Tips from ½ pound fresh
asparagus
½ teaspoon salt

2 tablespoons butter
2 tablespoons milk
1 egg
½ teaspoon lemon juice
2 tablespoons butter

Cook potatoes and asparagus separately until tender. Force vegetables through food mill. Season the purée with salt, 2 tablespoons butter and milk and blend until smooth. Beat the egg and add to the purée. Stuff the fish with the mixture and skewer it together. Place in a buttered baking dish, sprinkle with lemon juice and dot with remaining 2 tablespoons butter. Bake in moderate, 350° F., oven 25 minutes, or until fish flakes when tested with a fork. Makes 3 or 4 servings.

This is a later phase recipe.

MEAT

The choice of meat to cook and to eat is not so much limited as it is specialized. At first glance the basic varieties all seem to be included. However, we are limited to the top grades and to the simplified preparation.

The range encompasses beef, lamb, chicken as well as liver, brains and sweetbreads.

The steaks, chops, hamburger and chicken can be broiled. The other meat and the chicken can be prepared employing a wider range of cooking techniques.

I found that beef gave me the greatest variety of dishes. There are broiled steaks from porterhouse, sirloin, filet mignon and chuck steak fillet. There are also ground round steak and the different roasts of beef.

From lamb, we use the rib and loin chops.

Chicken breast and liver are in our diet and these offer inspiration for varied dishes.

So do calf's liver, brains, and sweetbreads and a great challenge to prepare and enjoy them.

For all of the above, the meat dealer can be a great help, guide and counsel. He can advise on the choice of cuts to avoid expensive beef, and he can suggest best ways of preparing meat, as well as ways to avoid waste in serving a family's needs.

The steaks, chops and ground meat all need careful trimming so that they will have a minimum of fat on them when they are cooked. I often found that I had to trim these meats myself before broiling the steak or chop I was to eat.

Broiled Beef

Cuts to buy:

Filet Mignon	Lean round steak, ground
Fillet of Chuck	or chopped
Porterhouse	Lean small Steaks: "Chicken
Sirloin	Steak," Rib Steak, T-Bone
	and so on

To broil, remove all fat and fatty tissue from meat. It is a wise idea to let meat reach room temperature before broiling, so try to take it from the refrigerator an hour or more before cooking it. Broil over charcoal or in range at a steady high heat, to the degree of doneness desired. Turn it once or twice. Do not season the meat before cooking. A little butter may be put on the cooked meat before serving.

During the later phase of the diet, a sprig of fresh herb may be laid across the meat while it cooks. Discard herb before serving. A handful of an aromatic herb thrown into burning charcoal is another subtle way of flavoring foods broiled on charcoal.

Lamb Chops

Select loin or rib chops. Carefully remove all fat.

Broil like steak but cook a little slower, over lower heat.

For later phase seasoning, broil with herbs. Fresh mint (which we normally avoid) is a pleasant herb to burn on the charcoal. A little of its tang will be carried into the meat with the charcoal-broiled flavor.

Roast Beef

Use only small, lean, boned roasts.

Do not sear meat or season it.

Place meat on rack in uncovered pan. Set pan in cold oven and start oven at moderate, 325° F. Roast about 20 minutes per pound for rare roast beef. Longer for medium. If your preference is for well-done beef, let the meat cook a little longer than for medium, but not really well-done. Count ¼ to ½ pound as 1 serving.

This is a later phase recipe.

Liver

Buy calf's, chicken, or lamb's liver. About ¼ to ⅓ pound is an average serving. Remove all tough membrane. Rinse, drain, wipe dry.

To broil: Dust lightly with flour and place under moderate broiler heat. Cook only until brown and crusty on each side. Do not cook until well-done.

Chicken livers or cubes of other liver may be charcoal broiled on skewers.

A little melted butter makes a pleasant dressing over broiled liver.

This is an early phase recipe.

Shepherd's Pie

2 medium potatoes, peeled
  and diced
½ teaspoon salt
2 to 3 tablespoons milk

2 tablespoons butter
1 pound lean ground steak
1 tablespoon water

Boil potatoes, drain and mash, adding salt, milk and butter to make creamy mashed potatoes. Butter a pie pan and use mashed potatoes to form a bottom "crust." Mix the meat with water and press it into a flat cake to cover the potatoes within about an inch of the top rim of the pan. Bake in a hot, 450° F., oven until the meat is done to taste, about 20 to 30 minutes. May be topped with poached eggs. Makes 2 servings.

This is a later phase recipe.

Sweetbreads

Sweetbreads must be soaked and parboiled before they can be used in a recipe. Soak in cold water to cover for several hours. Drain and add cold water again to cover with 1 teaspoon salt for each pair of sweetbreads. Bring water to a boil and simmer slowly 5 minutes. Drain and let cold water run over the breads to cool them. Trim connecting tubes and tough tissue.

Braised Sweetbreads

1 pair sweetbreads, parboiled
2 carrots, sliced

1 cup water
½ teaspoon salt
½ teaspoon lemon juice

Place carrot slices in a casserole, add water, salt and lemon juice. Lay the sweetbreads over the carrot. Cover the casserole and bake in a moderate, 375° F., oven 30 minutes. Uncover and continue baking another 30 minutes. The ulcer patient should not eat the cooked carrot or any sauce. He may put a little butter over the sweetbreads as they finish cooking. Makes 2 servings.

This is a later phase recipe.

Creamed Sweetbreads

1 pair sweetbreads,
    parboiled
2 tablespoons butter
1½ tablespoons flour
1 cup milk; heated

3 steamed mushroom caps,
    sliced thinly (optional)
½ teaspoon salt
1 egg yolk
3 tablespoons cream

Melt butter, add flour and cook 1 minute. Slowly add hot milk and stir over low heat until thick. Slice sweetbreads and add to cream sauce with mushrooms and salt. Cook, slowly, stirring frequently for 20 minutes. Mix egg yolk with cream and add to mixture. Cook, stirring constantly, for 3 more minutes. Serve on toast points. Makes 2 servings.

This is an early phase recipe.

Mousse au Cervelle (Calf's Brains)

1 pair calf's brains
1 teaspoon each salt and
 lemon juice
4 egg yolks
2 cups milk

½ teaspoon salt
2 envelopes gelatin
¼ cup cold water
¼ cup boiling water
2 cups heavy cream, whipped

Soak brains in cold water for one hour. Remove membranes and tubes. Drain the brains, put in cold water to cover, add salt and lemon juice and boil 15 minutes. Drain and press through food mill.

Beat egg yolks well, combine with milk in top of double boiler over hot water, beat and cook until mixture coats a spoon. Season with ½ teaspoon of salt. Soak gelatin in ¼ cup of cold water, add ¼ cup of boiling water to dissolve gelatin. Combine and blend all ingredients excepting cream. Let cool, add partially whipped cream. Place in a well buttered 1½ quart mold and let stand overnight in the refrigerator. Unmold and serve cold. Makes 3 or 4 servings.

This is an early phase recipe.

Calf's Brain Casserole

1 pair calf's brains
1 teaspoon each lemon juice
   and salt
½ cup each diced cooked
   potato and carrot

3 tablespoons butter, melted
½ teaspoon salt
3 tablespoons puréed spinach
   (may be baby food)

Soak brains in cold water for 1 hour. Drain, remove membranes and tubes. Place brains in cold water to cover, add salt and lemon juice and boil 15 minutes. Drain and slice into a casserole, add potatoes and carrots. Mix butter, salt and spinach into a "dressing" and toss brains and vegetables with it. Heat in moderate, 325° F., oven a few minutes, until heated through. Makes 2 servings.

This is an early phase recipe.

Beef Stroganoff

½ pound beef fillet
3 small carrots, cooked and
   shredded
2 tablespoons butter, melted

⅛ teaspoon salt
2 to 3 drops lemon juice
½ cup Cream Sauce
   (see recipe)

Broil the fillet but keep it very rare. Cut it into thin slices and arrange them with the shredded carrot in a heated shallow baking dish. Pour butter over meat and carrots, sprinkle with salt and lemon juice. Return to broiler for 1 minute. Add hot Cream Sauce, toss and serve immediately. Makes 1 or 2 servings.

This is a later phase recipe.

Calf's Liver Rolls

1 pound calf's liver, cut into
   4 slices
1 cup mashed potatoes
½ cup Pea Puree (see recipe)
2 tablespoons butter

2 tablespoons light cream
¼ teaspoon salt
1 egg
2 tablespoons butter, melted

Rinse and dry liver, place it between sheets of waxed paper and set a weight on it. Combine and thoroughly blend all other ingredients, excepting melted butter. Spread some of the purée mixture on each slice of liver and roll it up, secure with metal skewers. Broil liver rolls under medium heat, turning them several times to brown well all over. Remove rolls to heated plates, pour a little melted butter over them and serve immediately. Makes 3 or 4 servings.

This is a later phase recipe.

Fillet of Beef and Pâté

¾ pound beef fillet cut into
   2 strips
3 chicken livers

⅛ teaspoon salt
2 tablespoons butter, melted

Broil chicken livers 5 minutes, turning them frequently. Mash the livers into a paste with the salt. Spread 1 side of each piece of beef with paste, roll it and secure with a skewer or tie it. Broil under high heat until done but rare. Remove to a heated serving platter and pour melted butter over the steaks. Serve immediately. Makes 2 servings.

This is a later phase recipe.

Skewered Meat

Liver, steak or lamb, cut in cubes may be skewered and broiled over charcoal for an interesting change in flavor. Use tender lean cuts of meat and broil over a fire that has burned down to coals with a coating of white ash. Meat should be cooked only as long as necessary to serve rare.

Serve with cooked potatoes and carrots, diced and tossed with quantities of melted butter. You may toss the cooked cubes of meat with the vegetables and butter for a delicious melange. Count ¼ to ½ pound meat as 1 serving.

Poached Chicken

Chicken that is poached rather than boiled has much more flavor and a pleasanter texture. The dieter has no interest in soup or soup stock from his chicken, which is further reason to poach and not boil it. The more concentrated broth from the poaching can be useful to the cook in preparing dishes for other members of the family. The poached chicken is very useful for cold dishes or sandwiches.

1 whole chicken, 3 pounds,   1½ cups water
   broiler or fryer, cleaned and   1 teaspoon salt
   ready to cook

Place chicken in a roomy kettle with a tight lid, add water and salt, cover and bring water to a boil. Reduce heat and continue slow cooking or steaming 40 minutes. Chicken may also be steamed with a rack under it or in a pressure cooker. Makes 4 or more servings.

Variation:

To poach chicken breasts, whole or split, use ¼ teaspoon salt and ½ cup water for each. Steam for 20 minutes, test for doneness. Thick chicken breasts require longer cooking. One large breast makes 2 servings.

This is an early phase recipe.

Broiled Breast of Chicken

1 chicken breast, with skin removed

¼ teaspoon salt
1 teaspoon butter (optional)

Rinse chicken breast, wipe dry and sprinkle with salt. Place with skin side upon broiler rack. Broil under high heat, 450° F., 10 minutes on each side. For moister chicken, turn side up again, dot with butter and broil 1 minute longer. Orange Sauce (see recipe) will offer variety if added to the chicken. One large chicken breast split makes 2 servings.

This is an early phase recipe.

Breast of Chicken in Cream Sauce

2 chicken breasts, split but
    not boned
½ teaspoon salt
¾ cup water
2 tablespoons flour

2 tablespoons butter, melted
1 cup milk
1 cup diced cooked carrots
    and potatoes

Boil chicken in salted water 20 minutes. Remove chicken to warm platter. Combine flour, butter, and milk, and add slowly to the broth, stirring continually. Stir and cook until thickened. Heat potatoes and carrots in this sauce and pour all over the chicken breasts. Makes 2 to 4 servings.

As diet restrictions ease, chicken may be seasoned with a sprig of fresh tarragon or a few chives, and a minute dash of finely ground white pepper. The herbs should be removed before serving.

This is a later phase recipe.

Diced Beef Hash

½ pound lean trimmed steak ⅛ teaspoon salt
¼ cup cooked carrot, diced 2 tablespoons butter or oil
½ cup cooked potato, diced

Cut meat into tiny cubes. Mix the meat and vegetables in a baking dish and bake in a hot, 425° F., oven for 8 minutes. Add salt and butter, toss the meat and vegetables and place under broiler flame for 1 minute. Serve immediately.

This is a later phase recipe.

Beef Medallions

2 rounds of steak fillet of 3 to 1 tablespoon Special
4 ounces each Mayonnaise (see recipe) or
2 rounds of toast butter — optional

Broil steak 2 minutes each side on a sheet of foil in a 500° F. broiler. Put toast under steak to blot up drippings from foil and top with mayonnaise or butter and return to broiler for ½ minute longer.

This is a later phase recipe.

Tournedos Rossini

6-ounce fillet
1 toast round

1 chicken liver
1 tablespoon butter

Broil the chicken liver until done and mash it with the butter. Broil the steak for 2 minutes each side and place it on the toast. Spread the steak with the chicken liver paste and return to the broiler for ½ minute.

This is a later phase recipe.

Breast of Chicken Casserole

1 chicken breast
1 medium potato, diced
2 small carrots, diced
¼ teaspoon salt

1 cup water
2 tablespoons butter
⅛ teaspoon salt

Bake all the ingredients, saving the butter and second salt, in a covered casserole in a medium, 350° F., oven for 30 to 40 minutes. Drain the liquid, reserving about 1 tablespoon and peel the skin from the chicken breast. Add the tablespoon of cooking liquid, the butter, and remaining salt, toss and place under the broiler flame for 2 minutes.

This is a later phase recipe.

Chicken and Mushrooms

1 sliced breast of chicken
2 pieces toast, trimmed
4 steamed mushroom caps

1 tablespoon butter, softened
2 tablespoons Special
   Mayonnaise (see recipe)

Make a purée from ⅓ of the chicken, the mushrooms, butter, and mayonnaise. This may be done in the blender or with a mortar and pestle. Spread the purée on the toast, top with thinly sliced chicken. Heat for 4 to 5 minutes in a warm, 225° F., oven.

This is a later phase recipe.

Chicken Breast Rossini

1 sliced breast of cooked
   chicken
2 pieces of toast, trimmed and
   buttered

1 chicken liver
1 tablespoon butter

Broil the chicken liver and mash with the butter. Cover the toast with thinly sliced chicken and top with the mashed chicken liver. Broil for 1 minute.

This is an early phase recipe.

PASTA, RICE AND CEREAL

Grains, or the simple foods made from them can be the entire meal, the accompaniment, or the basis for the greatest gastronomical feats.

The amateur chef revels in his unrevealed secret recipe for spaghetti sauce. Later he may go on to a simpler but more painstaking manner for serving spaghetti: hot, perfectly cooked pasta, loads of sweet butter, salt, pepper and freshly grated Parmesan cheese.

We should spend the extra few pennies and the extra minutes for the proper preparation of grain foods. Buy good quality pasta and use whole grain rice, not the quick cook or regenerated varieties. Our "sauces" are simple and the clean nut-like taste of the grain foods will be the dominant flavor, so enjoy them at their best.

PASTA

Pasta, or paste, comes in many forms, shapes and sizes. I recommend the simpler, thinner ones for the dieter. They taste better with the sauce substitutes than lasagna without cheese. From baby grains of pastine to mammoth macaroni and with noodles and spaghetti, there is a goodly roster of pasta to choose from. Although they are basically made from the same ingredients, somehow each shape has its unique flavor.

Pasta should be cooked fresh for each meal. It should be tender but not overcooked and pasty. Serve it in soups or in Oyster Stew (see recipe). A good quality of spaghetti with lots of melted butter makes a marvelous accompaniment to steak. This should make you forget the overly spiced sauce concoctions of the past.

Pasta "Sauces"

Early Phase

Butter, margarine, salad oil
Vegetable purées
Cottage cheese

Cream cheese
Warm milk or cream

See sauce recipes, pages 143-149

Later Phase

Olive oil
Herb Butters (see recipes)

Tomato Purée (see recipe)

Spinach Noodles

¼ pound noodles
½ pound fresh (or frozen)
   young spinach
1 quart boiling water

½ teaspoon salt
3 tablespoons butter
3 tablespoons cottage cheese

Cook the spinach and noodles in the boiling, salted water for 12 minutes. Drain, but do not discard all of the water. Heat ½ cup of the cooking water with the butter and cheese. Toss the noodles and the sauce and serve immediately. Makes 2 servings.

This is an early phase recipe.

Pilaf

¼ cup rice
¼ cup thin spaghetti, broken
    into pieces

1 quart vegetable juices (see
    suggestion for saving same)
½ teaspoon salt
2 tablespoons butter

Cook rice and spaghetti in salted vegetable juice (you may add water to less than 1 quart of juice) until done. Drain and return pilaf to cooking pot, heat over low heat for 1 minute to dry, then add butter and heat, tossing pilaf for 1 more minute. Makes 2 servings.

This is a later phase recipe.

Macaroni and Chicken Livers

1 serving cooked macaroni
¼ pound chicken livers

2 tablespoons Herb Butter
    (chive or tarragon)
¼ teaspoon salt

Broil whole chicken livers to rare stage and dice them. Heat and salt butter and toss chicken livers over low heat for 1 minute. Pour over macaroni.

This is a later phase recipe.

Spaghetti Tartare

1 serving cooked thin
  spaghetti
¼ pound lean steak, finely
  chopped

2 tablespoons Herb Butter
  (chive)
¼ teaspoon salt

Heat butter, add salt and steak and toss over low heat for 1 minute. Pour over spaghetti and serve immediately.

This is a later phase recipe.

Hot Macaroni Salad

1 serving cooked macaroni
¼ cup thin Cream Sauce
  (see recipe)

1 cup mixed vegetables (tiny
  peas, cooked diced carrots,
  diced avocado)
⅛ teaspoon salt
2 to 3 drops lemon juice

Heat the vegetables in the cream sauce for 1 minute, season with salt and lemon juice and pour over the macaroni. Serve immediately.

This is a later phase recipe.

RICE

There are many ways to cook rice. What is important is not how it is cooked but that the grains remain separated. These recipes are for whole-grain rice; the converted rice should be cooked following package directions.

1 cup rice	½ teaspoon salt
1¾ cups water	1 tablespoon butter or oil

Wash rice thoroughly. Put in a heavy pan with the other ingredients, cover tightly and bring to a boil. Stir once, cover and simmer 14 to 16 minutes. Rice should be dry with all water absorbed.

Another method is to cook it until tender in 2 quarts of water per cupful of rice. When tender, drain and rinse the rice in cold water, then dry it over very low heat or in a warm oven until the grains separate. Cooked rice, if covered, will keep well in the refrigerator. 1 cup of dry rice cooked makes 3 to 4 servings.

Rice "Sauces"

Rice may be served with the same "sauces" as pasta. Cooked rice is also good with fruit or jelly and warm cream as a luncheon main course.

My Special Pilaf

½ cup rice
½ cup thin spaghetti, broken
   into short pieces

2 cups water
1 teaspoon salt
¼ pound butter (1 stick)

Cook rice and spaghetti in salted water until rice is tender. If rice is not sufficiently cooked by the time all the water has been absorbed add more water a little at a time until the rice is cooked. The spaghetti will be cooked before the rice, so watch the rice only. When the rice is done add the butter and cook, stirring and tossing for 1 minute. The starch that has cooked off the rice and spaghetti becomes the sauce with the butter. Makes 2 servings.

This is a later phase recipe.

Rice and Mushrooms

1 serving cooked rice
¼ cup rich Cream Sauce
   (see recipe)

4 steamed mushroom caps
⅛ teaspoon salt

Chop steamed mushrooms fairly fine and heat in cream sauce with salt. Pour sauce over rice and serve hot.

This is a later phase recipe.

Rice and Puréed Peas

1 serving cooked rice
1 small can early June peas,
   drained
1½ tablespoons butter, melted

⅛ tablespoon salt
2 tablespoons parsley
2 tablespoons light cream

Place all ingredients in blender and blend at high speed for 1 minute. Heat purée over low heat and serve over the rice.

This is a later phase recipe.

Vegetable Rice Pudding

¼ cup rice
  2 small carrots, scraped and
    diced
¼ cup chopped spinach
  1 zucchini, peeled and sliced

¼ teaspoon salt
2 cups water
2 tablespoons butter
½ cup milk

Cook rice in salted water for 5 minutes, add vegetables and cook 5 minutes longer. Drain and place in covered baking dish with butter and milk. Bake in moderate, 350° F., oven for 30 minutes. Makes 2 servings.

This is a later phase recipe.

CEREAL

Our cereals are cream of wheat or cream of rice, farina, and oatmeal. The usual accompaniments are milk, cream, butter and white or brown sugar. Maple sugar, syrups and jellies may be served in the cereal or fresh peaches.

Cooked cereal can be an agreeable change from potatoes; use cereal as the starchy dish in a meal.

For a soup garnish, allow the cooked cereal (a good use for any that is left over from breakfast) to get thick and cold in a small shallow bowl, cut into cubes and drop them into hot soup just before serving.

Cottage Cheese Dumplings

Can be used as main course or soup garnish.

½ pound of creamed cottage
  cheese
4 tablespoons bread crumbs
2 eggs

1 tablespoon cold water
½ teaspoon salt (late in diet
  pinch of white pepper
  and/or nutmeg)

Mash cottage cheese and bread crumbs until thoroughly blended. Beat eggs and water until frothy. Add eggs and salt to cheese and blend well. Place bowl in refrigerator and bring a large pot full of slightly salted water to a rolling boil. Drop dumpling mixture into boiling water a scant teaspoonful at a time, keep water boiling slowly adding dumplings. Cover and reduce heat, but keep water boiling for 5 minutes. Remove dumplings with a slotted spoon, and serve immediately. Can be served with vegetable purées or in creamed soup or tomato bouillon. Makes 3 or 4 servings.

This is an early phase recipe.

Oatmeal Soufflé

½ cup cooked thin oatmeal   2 eggs, separated
½ cup milk, heated   ⅛ teaspoon salt, or less
 2 tablespoons butter

Combine the oatmeal, milk, and butter and blend thoroughly.
Beat the egg yolks with the salt and mix into oatmeal mixture;
fold in stiffly beaten egg whites. Turn into a well-buttered baking
dish, set in a pan of hot water and bake in a moderate, 350° F.,
oven 45 minutes. Makes 2 servings.

This is an early phase recipe.

VEGETABLES

Sound cooking methods must be followed when preparing vegetables for purée to realize every bit of their inherent flavor. Steaming or pressure cooking and careful timing are essential. The foods cooked this way will retain so many of their natural flavors and salts that the lack of added seasoning will not be missed.

Save the vegetable juices from the steaming. They are tonic when taken as a beverage. They are useful in cooking. Keep a few large jars with tight lids handy, pour the juices into the jars and store in the refrigerator. The juices from canned vegetables (often the best part) should also be saved.

A *Note on Preparation*

Steam cooking of vegetables, known for many centuries to the Chinese (and the reason for the fresh flavor of many of their well-prepared dishes) is not a cooking mystery nor is it difficult to do. It simply means not immersing the food directly into water, but letting the steam from boiling water do the cooking.

You will need a pressure cooker with a rack; or a heavy pot with a tight lid and a steamer rack. I usually use a steamer rack that costs about a dollar. It is made of aluminum with little folding legs and perforated petals. I place it in a kettle, and pour water in only to just below the top of the rack.

To steam food, place the vegetables on the rack, cover and bring water to a boil. Water must continue boiling to create steam; cook for required time. Or follow the directions on your pressure cooker or steamer.

Baked Potatoes

Scrub and oil skin (although you should not eat the skin). Bake in a moderate oven, 350° F., until soft. To test for softness, protect fingers with folded towel, and press potato gently. Potatoes will adapt themselves to the heat of an oven set for another food, excepting a high-heat oven. When done, if not to be served immediately, pierce skin with a fork to release steam, and they will not shrivel and grow soggy.

Baked potatoes can be served in a variety of ways. Scoop the contents from the shells and mix with cream and butter. There will be a slight flavor difference if mashed smoothly or coarsely. Try them with margarine or olive oil. Then heap the potato mixture back into the shells.

Mash them with butter and a tablespoon or so of vegetable juice or purée. Or with finely diced cooked carrots.

This is an early phase recipe.

Baked Potatoes and Herb Cream

2 large baking potatoes,
  scrubbed
½ cup cream

3 tablespoons Herb Butter
  (chive) (see recipe)
¼ teaspoon salt

Bake potatoes until soft. Cut long slice from skin across length of each potato. Scoop out meat and mash with cream, and Herb Butter. Stuff potato skins loosely with mixture and reheat in the oven for 3 to 4 minutes. Dieter should not eat potato skin. Makes 2 servings.

This is a later phase recipe.

Baked Potatoes and Mushrooms

2 large baking potatoes
6 medium mushroom caps
½ cup water

¼ cup heavy cream
3 tablespoons butter (can be
  herb butter)

Scrub, oil, and bake potatoes. Steam mushroom caps in covered pan 10 minutes over ½ cup of water. Mince mushrooms very fine and add to cream and butter in small saucepan. Heat thoroughly, but do not cook mixture.

Cut baked potatoes lengthwise and carefully scoop out the contents. Mash the potato with the mushroom mixture and refill the skins. Heat for a few minutes in moderate, 325° F., oven. Makes 2 servings.

This is a later phase recipe.

Boiled Potatoes

The thin–skinned new potatoes are best boiled or steamed in their skins in or above lightly salted water. Peel them after they are cooked. To my taste they are the best flavored potatoes. Before peeling them, try toasting them for a minute in the cooking pan: pour off all the water in which they cooked and toss them gently in the pot over medium heat.

Slice or dice the cooked potatoes and douse them with butter, margarine, or oil. Try them with cottage cheese, or even whipped cream, and a sprinkle of salt.

This is an early phase recipe.

Mashed Potatoes

Potatoes   Butter, margarine, or olive oil
Water   Cream or milk
Salt

Peel and cut the potatoes. Boil them in lightly salted water to cover, but don't drown them, until they are soft but not mushy. Pour off water and dry them by shaking the pan over the heat. Mash them in the pan and add butter and cream, or oil and vegetable juice, to obtain the desired consistency. Beat until fluffy. Count 1 large or 2 small potatoes for each serving.

This is an early phase recipe.

Potato Casserole

2 medium potatoes, unpeeled
2 to 3 small carrots, scraped
1 cup water
2 tablespoons butter (for later
    diet phase try herb butter)

¼ cup light cream
½ cup cottage cheese
¼ teaspoon salt

Cook vegetables separately or steam together, adding carrots (whole) 5 minutes or so after potatoes have begun to steam. (This last cannot be done if you are using a pressure cooker.) You must judge the cooking time according to the size of the potatoes and the youth of the carrots. When potatoes are cooked, peel and dice them; slice cooked carrots into thin discs.

Melt butter in small baking dish, add cream, and heat, adding cottage cheese and vegetables. Season with salt and heat thoroughly, but do not allow to cook. Serve hot. Makes 2 servings.

This is an early phase recipe.

Mashed Potatoes and Carrots

2 large potatoes, peeled	3 tablespoons butter
½ pound carrots, scraped	¼ teaspoon salt
½ cup light cream	1 egg yolk

Cook potatoes and carrots separately in lighly salted water. Drain the vegetables and mash them fine. Add the other ingredients and beat until smooth. Beat over low heat until just hot. Makes 2 generous servings.

This is an early phase recipe.

Carrot-Potato Puffs

½ cup diced cooked carrots	1 egg
1 cup diced cooked potatoes	2 to 3 tablespoons milk or
½ teaspoon salt	cream
2 tablespoons butter	

Mash carrots and potatoes together. Add salt, butter (melted, if vegetables are cold), and egg. Blend all ingredients thoroughly. Add milk or cream, using judgment as to the quantity so as to make a thick, doughy mixture. Use a large spoon or an ice cream scoop to drop mixture onto a lightly greased cookie sheet. Bake in a pre-heated hot oven, 450° F., for 5 to 10 minutes. Timing is important: the puffs should be softer than the ones for normal diet. They should not be baked until firm and dry. Remove from the sheet with a spatula and serve hot. Makes 4 servings.

This is a later phase recipe.

VEGETABLES TO PURÉE

There are 3 primary methods for our purée. I will specify where each is best used.

Mashing. This can be done with a fork, potato masher, ricer, or through a sieve. This method is for soft foods which have no pulp.

Blending. Using an electric blender and all the food, usually with the juices. For foods which have little pulp or fibers and such as they do have can be safely eaten. This is a quick and handy method, and the blender is well worth its cost.

Food mill. Makes true purée. The fibers and tough parts are screened out and only the essence remains. As in the case with the blender, ease and speed are gained with the use of this inexpensive tool. A fine sieve can be used, but the above methods are preferred.

GREEN PEAS

Purée of Green Peas I

1 pound early peas in the pod,
  or 1 (8- to 10-oz.) package
  frozen early peas

½ cup water
⅛ teaspoon salt

Bring water to boil under steamer rack in heavy saucepan with tightly fitted lid. Add shelled peas (or frozen), sprinkle with salt and steam 8 to 10 minutes (5 to 6 for frozen peas). Pour cooking water and peas into blender and blend at high speed until smooth. The purée will have a richer taste if you add 2 table-spoons of butter or heavy cream. This recipe makes 3 to 4 serv-ings. It will keep well if covered for a few days in the refrigerator.

This is an early phase recipe.

Note: Canned early June peas may be used for a short cut and to make a smaller amount of purée. Pour the entire contents of the smallest size can into the blender and blend until smooth.
Purée may be heated in a double boiler or in custard cups placed in a little simmering water in a shallow pan.

Purée of Green Peas II

1 medium to large size potato,   3 tablespoons milk
  cooked and diced   ⅛ tablespoon salt
2 tablespoons butter

Prepare pea purée as above. Reserve one serving from blender. Add potato, or two cooked, diced carrots, and other ingredients and blend until smooth. Fill individual serving dishes. Oven-proof glass custard cups are particularly useful. Cover with foil and store in refrigerator. To heat, place cups in simmering water in shallow pan. Makes 3 servings.

This is an early phase recipe.

For later phase variations, add a few tender lettuce leaves to the peas before they are put into the blender. Or steam them with a sprig of fresh herb (dill or tarragon is good), but remember to discard the herb before blending the peas.

Early Garden Peas with Lettuce

1 pound shelled peas   ⅛ teaspoon salt
3 to 4 Boston lettuce leaves   ¼ cup water
1 teaspoon sugar   2 to 3 tablespoons butter

Lay lettuce leaves in bottom of heavy saucepan with tight lid. Add water, peas, sugar, and salt. Cover and cook over medium heat for 5 to 7 minutes. Drain liquid and remove lettuce, add butter and heat until melted. Makes 2 to 3 servings.

This is a later phase recipe.

STRING BEANS AND WAX BEANS

I found that the flavor of these when puréed is rather bitter. However, if the purée is added to other vegetables, the flavor improves. The beans should be young and tender; unless you grow your own or can buy from a good vegetable market, it is best to use frozen beans.

String Bean Purée

1 (8- to 10-oz.) package
  frozen string beans
½ cup water
⅛ teaspoon salt

½ cup diced cooked potatoes,
  carrots, or squash
2 tablespoons butter

Bring water to boil under steamer rack in tightly covered pan. Add beans and steam 8 to 10 minutes. Reserve liquid and set aside 2 servings of the beans (this for family members not on diet). Force third serving of the beans and the other vegetable through a food mill. Add butter and 1 or 2 tablespoons of the cooking liquid from the beans, or milk, if mixture is too thick. (Add rest of cooking liquid to refrigerator jar of vegetable juices if you are saving these.) Makes 3 to 4 servings.

This is an early phase recipe.

TOMATOES

You should eat neither the skin nor the seeds of tomatoes. (The consumption of this vegetable should be limited in our diet because it is fairly high in acid content.)

Tomato Purée

2 to 3 ripe tomatoes,
   quartered
¼ cup water

1 teaspoon sugar
⅛ teaspoon salt

Place all ingredients in covered pan and simmer 15 minutes. Force all pulp and juice through a food mill. This should make about 1 cup of purée. It may be eaten hot or cold, making about 1 serving. Or the purée will prove useful as a simple sauce, or added to other cooked foods.

This is a later phase recipe.

Tomato Mousse

½ cup Tomato Purée
  (see recipe)
¼ teaspoon salt
 2 to 3 drops lemon juice
½ cup Special Mayonnaise
  (see recipe)

1 envelope gelatin
2 tablespoons water (1 warm,
  1 hot)
½ cup heavy cream, whipped
  until stiff

Mix tomato purée, salt, lemon juice, and mayonnaise thoroughly. Soften gelatin in 1 tablespoon warm water and stir in the 1 tablespoon of hot water to dissolve the gelatin. Add gelatin and whipped cream to tomato mixture and blend thoroughly. Pour into a small mold or custard cups. Chill until firm. Makes 2 servings.

This is a later phase recipe.

ASPARAGUS

I prefer to eat asparagus when it is in season, although the frozen or canned varieties can be substituted for the fresh vegetable. Always try to choose asparagus that is of one thickness, thin or thick. The tips cook much faster than the stalks, and judging cooking time is difficult enough without finding an average for spears of different weights.

Purée of Asparagus Tips

1 pound asparagus broken
   into about 5- to 6-in. tips
½ cup water

⅛ teaspoon salt
2 tablespoons butter or
   heavy cream

Bring water to a boil under steamer rack in a pan with tight lid.
Lay asparagus tips on rack, sprinkle with salt and steam until
tender, at least 10 minutes. Pour cooking liquid and asparagus
into food mill and force through. Add butter or cream and heat
until smooth. Serve hot. Makes 2 servings.

This is an early phase recipe.

Asparagus Soufflé

2 tablespoons butter
1 tablespoon flour
1 cup hot milk
½ cup Asparagus Purée
   (see recipe)

3 egg yolks, slightly beaten
3 egg whites, beaten stiff
¼ teaspoon salt

Melt butter in a saucepan, add flour, and cook 1 minute. Add hot
milk and cook, stirring constantly, until thick and smooth. Add
asparagus purée and continue heating and stirring until it reaches
the boiling point. Remove from heat and add egg yolks, blend
mixture, and fold into stiffly beaten egg whites. Fill a well-buttered, 1-quart deep baking dish no more than ¾ full of mixture
and set in a moderate oven, 350° to 375° F. Bake 30 to 40 minutes. Top should rise to a high crown and should brown lightly.
Serve at once. Makes 2 servings.

This is an early phase recipe.

Broccoli

This vegetable, good fresh or frozen, is between string beans and asparagus in our diet. It is good puréed alone, but it lends itself well to blends with other vegetables. It requires, as does cauliflower (which we dare not eat), careful cooking; even if we are to purée broccoli it should not be cooked until the flowerets fall off the stems.

1 small bunch broccoli,   ½ cup water
   trimmed (or 1 8- to 10-oz.   ⅛ teaspoon salt
   package frozen)   2 tablespoons butter

Wash broccoli, look over, cut in small pieces. Bring water to a boil in a covered saucepan containing a steamer rack. Place broccoli on rack, sprinkle with salt and steam until tender, about 8 minutes. Force broccoli and cooking liquid through food mill. Add butter and mix until smooth. Serve hot. Makes 2 servings.

This vegetable mixes well with potatoes or squash.

This is a later phase recipe.

BEETS

Use very young, small beets only.

Baked Baby Beets

Trim and scrub several small beets. Place them in a pan with a little water to prevent scorching, and bake in a slow, 300° F., oven 30 minutes. Drain, peel, and mash beets with butter to taste.

Add a few small cooked beets to potatoes that are to be mashed in the blender or through the food mill. They will add a rather shocking color, but also a pleasant taste.

This is a later phase recipe.

SPINACH

The prepared baby food or junior baby food of puréed spinach is a very helpful substitute for puréed fresh spinach.

Purée of Spinach

1 pound tender young spinach	⅛ teaspoon salt
½ cup water	½ cup hot Cream Sauce (see recipe)

Pick over, remove thick stems and wash the spinach thoroughly. Cook in salted water in a tightly covered pot until tender, about 8 to 10 minutes. Force cooking liquid and spinach through food mill and add to Cream Sauce. Blend until smooth. Serve hot. Makes 2 servings.

This is an early phase recipe.

SPINACH — VARIATIONS

The puréed spinach may be souffléd. Substitute spinach for asparagus (see Asparagus Soufflé recipe), and proceed.

Another variant is to substitute Special Mayonnaise for Cream Sauce (see Purée of Spinach and Special Mayonnaise recipes), and add 2 hard-cooked eggs, coarsely chopped, and heat. Makes 2 servings.

This is a later phase recipe.

MUSHROOMS

Mushrooms should be fresh, small in size (and number consumed), and stemmed.

Purée of Mushrooms

Caps from ¼ pound
   mushrooms
½ cup water
⅛ teaspoon salt

3 tablespoons to ½ cup light
   cream
1 tablespoon butter

Bring water to boil under steamer rack in pan with tight lid. Place mushroom caps on steamer and cook 12 minutes. Discard cooking liquid. Put cream (amount will vary according to use for mushroom purée, less for thick, more for thin) in blender and add mushroom caps. Blend at high speed until mushrooms are thoroughly chopped. Add butter and salt and continue blending until smooth. Serve as a vegetable or as a sauce. Makes 2 servings.

This is a later phase recipe.

Stuffed Mushroom Caps

12 steamed mushroom caps
   prepared as in recipe for
   purée
 1 cup diced, cooked potatoes

3 or more tablespoons butter
  (can be herb butter)
2 tablespoons heavy cream
¼ teaspoon salt

Prepare steamed mushroom caps. Prepare mashed potatoes from other ingredients. Make the potatoes very loose and buttery. Fill mushroom caps with potatoes, place in shallow pan, and heat thoroughly in moderate, 325° F., oven. Makes 2 or more servings.

This is a later phase recipe.

SQUASH

Hubbard, acorn, summer, and zucchini squash are the best known varieties. For our diet, they are all quite fibrous, and should be puréed or mashed without skins and seeds.

Hubbard Squash Purée

1 squash, scrubbed but whole
2 tablespoons butter

1 tablespoon brown sugar
⅛ teaspoon salt

Place the squash in a shallow pan, add a few tablespoons water to prevent scorching. Bake in moderate, 350° F., oven about 40 minutes, or until the squash feels soft. Remove from oven, cut, remove seeds and rind, and mash the pulp. There should be about 2 cups. Add the other ingredients and mash and blend well. Serve hot. Makes 3 or 4 servings.

This is a later phase recipe.

Purée of Zucchini

2 small zucchini, or 1 medium
   summer squash, cut into
   pieces
¼ cup water

1 tablespoon butter
1 teaspoon flour
1 cup hot milk
⅛ teaspoon salt

Steam zucchini over boiling water 8 minutes. Reserve liquid for refrigerator jar. Force zucchini through food mill and set aside.

Melt butter, add flour, stir and cook 1 minute, add milk and salt, stirring; cook until thick and smooth. Add zucchini and heat. Makes 2 small servings.

This is a later phase recipe.

Carrots Vichy

4 small carrots, scraped and
   thinly sliced
2 Boston lettuce leaves
2 teaspoons sugar

⅛ teaspoon salt
¾ cup water
2 tablespoons butter

Lay lettuce in the bottom of a saucepan and add carrots, salt, sugar, and water. Cook at a rolling boil until carrots are very tender and most of the water has evaporated. Remove lettuce, drain any remaining liquid, and add butter. Cook, tossing carrots to coat with the butter for 1 minute.

This is an early phase recipe.

SAUCES

In the true meaning of the word, the recipes that follow are not strictly what they claim to be. They are substitutes listed under this designation for lack of other terms for our diet.

Our sauces are unblessed by spice. Their purpose in our diet is to counter the dryness and vary the flavor of the foods we are allowed.

Orange Sauce

This is a chicken or meat sauce, not to be confused with dessert sauces.

½ cup orange juice
½ teaspoon cornstarch
¼ teaspoon salt

1 tablespoon butter
1 tablespoon white raisins
  (optional)

Stir cornstarch in the cold orange juice until dissolved. Cook over low heat, stirring constantly until juice is thick and clear. Season with salt, add butter and raisins, and cook for 1 minute longer. Let stand 5 minutes or longer, and keep it warm to allow raisins to soften. Serve warm. Makes a little more than ½ cup sauce.

This is a later phase recipe.

Herb Butters

Any of the following nine herbs may be used. However, preferences, as well as doctor's orders, should be the guide. Parsley, basil, and tarragon were the first ones I used when my diet began to expand. Chives were about the last, because of their relationship to onions. Caution should be your strongest guide.

Basil, chervil, chives, dill weed, parsley, rosemary, sage, summer savory, and tarragon are my nine herbs. I always try to use fresh herbs rather than dried ones.

¼ pound sweet butter (1 stick)
  1 sprig or a small bunch of
    herbs (single herb or a

mixture of no more than 3)
Boiling water

Melt butter over very low heat. Steep herbs in the melted butter, mashing them with a fork for a minute or two. Or plunge the herbs into boiling water, remove immediately and shake dry, proceed as before. Strain the butter through cheesecloth, and store in a covered bowl or jar in the refrigerator.

These are later phase recipes.

Note: Where I call for butter, I always mean sweet butter. This is essential for herb butters.

Basic Cream (or White) Sauce

2 tablespoons butter
2 tablespoons flour

1 cup hot milk or light cream
(or a mixture of both)

Melt butter and stir flour in slowly over low heat. For our diet we must cook the mixture less than is customary in making this sauce; stir about 1 minute. Add the milk slowly, stirring. Cook and stir until thick and smooth. Makes 1 cup sauce.

Variations

To make the Cream Sauce thinner or thicker, use more or less liquid.

A rich Cream Sauce is made by beating 1 or 2 egg yolks, and adding to the completed sauce. Usually 1 egg yolk is sufficient for this small amount of sauce.

These are early phase recipes.

Mushroom Sauce I

Caps from ¼ pound
    mushrooms
½ cup water

2 tablespoons butter
2 tablespoons light cream
⅛ teaspoon salt

Steam mushroom caps over boiling water 10 minutes. Discard cooking liquid. Melt butter, mix with cream, pour into blender. Add mushrooms a few at a time, blending at low speed. Season with salt and blend at high speed until smooth. If sauce is too thick, add a little more cream. Makes about ¾ cup sauce. Use with meat, fish, or spaghetti.

This is a later phase recipe.

Mushroom Sauce II

Caps from ¼ pound
    mushrooms
½ cup Cream Sauce

2 tablespoons butter, melted
⅛ teaspoon salt

Steam mushrooms over boiling water 10 minutes. Make Cream Sauce (see recipe). Put mushroom caps, Cream Sauce, melted butter, and salt in blender and turn to high speed. Blend until smooth. Makes about 1 cup sauce. Serve with noodles or rice.

This is a later phase recipe.

Tomato-Avocado Catchup

1 ripe avocado	3 tablespoons olive oil
¼ cup Tomato Purée	2 to 3 drops lemon juice
(see recipe)	⅛ teaspoon salt

Peel and pit avocado. Mash all ingredients together to blend thoroughly. Or use the electric blender. Store in tightly covered container in refrigerator. Use within few days. Makes about 1 cup catchup. Serve with broiled meat or fish.

This is a later phase recipe.

Tomato Cream Sauce

3 tablespoons Herb Butter	1 cup hot milk
(tarragon and/or basil	3 tablespoons Tomato Purée
are good)	(see recipe)
2 tablespoons flour	¼ teaspoon salt

Melt butter in saucepan over very low heat. Stir in flour and cook 1 minute, stirring constantly. Gradually add hot milk and continue stirring. Add tomato purée and salt, keep stirring and cook until thick and smooth. Makes about 1½ cups sauce. Use as spaghetti sauce.

This is a later phase recipe.

Oyster Cream Sauce

2 tablespoons butter (for later phase try dill butter)
1 tablespoon flour
½ cup light cream, heated

3 oysters, minced with their liquid
⅛ teaspoon salt

Melt butter, stir flour in and cook 1 minute, stirring constantly. Gradually add hot cream and stir until smooth, add oysters and salt and cook about 2 minutes. Sauce should be smooth and not very thick. Serve with rice or over poached fish. Makes about 1 cup sauce.

This is an early phase recipe.

Crumb Sauce

¼ cup bread crumbs
4 tablespoons butter, melted

1 hard-cooked egg yolk, mashed
⅛ teaspoon salt

Spread bread crumbs in a shallow pan, toast in a slow oven, 300° F., until dry and beginning to brown. Add melted butter, egg yolk, and salt, mix thoroughly and use to top buttered noodles. Makes about ¾ cup.

This is an early phase recipe.

Cold Sauce

1 cup Special Mayonnaise
  (see recipe)

1 envelope gelatin
¼ cup water

Soften gelatin in cold water for several minutes. Place over hot water and stir until the gelatin dissolves. Add mayonnaise and mix thoroughly. Let cool. Makes 1½ cups sauce.

This sauce is to coat cold chicken or fish, or is used to bind mixtures that are to be molded.

This is an early phase recipe.

Avocado Mayonnaise

1 egg
1 ripe avocado, peeled and
  diced

4 tablespoons olive oil
2 to 3 drops lemon juice
⅛ teaspoon salt

Break egg into the container of electric blender. Turn switch to high speed, turn off immediately and add all other ingredients. Turn blender on to high speed again, blend until mixture is smooth and thick. Can be used in place of our Special Mayonnaise. Keeps covered in refrigerator 4 days. Makes 1¼ cups mayonnaise.

This is a later phase recipe.

SALADS

Like the sauces, these are substitutes for the real thing, since they are lacking the ingredients — lettuce, celery, endive — that we normally associate with salads. They do, however, fulfill the same purpose. They are light, cooling dishes that make for good summertime meals or as accompaniments to more formal dinners.

Potato Salad

2 pounds new potatoes
½ teaspoon salt

½ cup Special Mayonnaise
(see recipe)
½ teaspoon salt

Scrub potatoes (do not peel them), rinse, drain. Boil in water to cover, seasoned with ½ teaspoon of salt. When tender, drain and set aside to cool. Peel the potatoes and slice or dice them, sprinkle with ½ teaspoon salt and toss lightly with mayonnaise. Chill. Makes 4 ample servings. Potato salad keeps well a day or two if tightly covered and stored in refrigerator.

This is a later phase recipe.

Variations:

Dice 1 ripe avocado and toss as above with potatoes and ¾ cup mayonnaise.

Chop 4 hard-cooked eggs coarsely and toss as above with ¾ cup mayonnaise.

Chicken Salad

1 poached chicken breast	⅛ teaspoon salt
(see Poached Chicken recipe)	¼ cup Special Mayonnaise
2 hard-cooked eggs	(see recipe)

Remove all skin and bones from chicken and dice the meat. Chop eggs into coarse pieces and combine with chicken, salt, and mayonnaise. Toss until well blended. Chill. Serve cold. Makes 2 servings.

This is a later phase recipe.

Variations:

Substitute ½ cup cooked carrots or 1 avocado, diced, for the eggs and proceed as above.

Chop the mixture very fine, and use as sandwich filling.

Or mince the chicken and egg yolks and stuff the mixture into the white halves of the egg.

Fruit Salad

1 ripe peach	2 tablespoons Special
1 ripe pear	Mayonnaise (see recipe)
	2 tablespoons orange juice

Peel peach and pear, remove stone and core and dice. (A simple method to peel peaches — plunge them into boiling water for 1 minute, skin will pull off very easily if the fruit is ripe.) Blend mayonnaise and orange juice and pour over the diced fruit. Chill. Serve cold. Makes 2 small servings.

This is a later phase recipe.

Variations:

Apricots, bananas, cooked apples, and avocados may be added or substituted. Heavy cream may be used for the mayonnaise. Other fruit juice and a drop of lemon juice may be used for the orange juice.

If canned fruit is used, make the dressing with a little of the syrup and a drop of lemon juice.

Chef's Salad

½ cup diced cold cooked
  potatoes
¼ cup large curd cottage
  cheese
¼ cup diced cooked chicken
  or cold cooked steak
 2 steamed mushroom caps,
  finely chopped

¼ cup diced cooked carrots, or
  peeled avocado, or tiny
  steamed peas
3 tablespoons olive oil
1 sprig fresh dill or tarragon
1 teaspoon lemon juice

Toss all ingredients with the olive oil except for the dill and lemon juice. Crush the dill into the lemon juice and let steep 15 minutes. Remove the dill and toss the lemon juice with the salad. Season with ⅛ teaspoon salt, if needed. Makes 1 large serving, or 2 small servings.

This is a later phase recipe.

Fruit and Cheese

¼ cup drained cooked peaches
¼ cup drained cooked prunes
 2 ounces (4 leveled
  tablespoons) cream cheese

2 tablespoons light cream
2 tablespoons prune juice

Cut peaches and prunes into small pieces and arrange on a salad plate. Mash the cream cheese with the cream and prune juice and spoon over the fruit. Serve with saltines. Makes 1 serving.

This is an early phase recipe.

Variations:

Other fruits (consult list) and cottage cheese may be substituted for the above.

ASPICS

We cannot use the raw, crisp vegetables usually found in aspic salads, but we can enjoy the jellied molds. I have already mentioned the wisdom of saving the juices from steamed, cooked, or canned vegetables; these are excellent to use as the stock for aspic. I keep the vegetable juice in a screw-top covered jar in the refrigerator, adding to it every time I cook a vegetable. It can be a refreshing beverage, or useful in cooking.

The aspic recipes make two servings, or they can be put into individual molds and used on successive days.

Eggs in Aspic

4 poached eggs
1 envelope gelatin
2 tablespoons cold water
1½ cups hot vegetable juice
⅛ teaspoon salt (optional)

2 to 3 drops lemon juice (at
    later phase of diet only)
½ cup heavy cream
⅛ teaspoon salt, or less

Poach eggs, trim excess whites and set aside to cool. Soften gelatin in cold water and add to hot vegetable juice, season with salt, if necessary (and lemon juice). Let gelatin cool until it begins to set. Pour a little of the gelatin into each of 2 individual molds and carefully arrange 2 poached eggs in each mold. Cover the eggs with the rest of the gelatin and chill in refrigerator for at least 2 hours.

At serving time, whip cream until stiff and season with a little salt. Unmold aspic and top with whipped cream. Makes 2 servings.

This is an early phase recipe.

Tomato Aspic

1½ cups Tomato Purée (see recipe)
1 envelope gelatin

2 tablespoons cold water
⅛ teaspoon salt
2 to 3 drops lemon juice

Soften gelatin in cold water and add to hot Tomato Purée. Season with salt and lemon juice, pour into 2 individual molds, let cool, and then chill. Makes 2 servings.

Variation:

½ ripe avocado, peeled and diced

¼ cup diced cooked carrots

Add the avocado and carrots to the Tomato Purée and gelatin. Complete recipe as given above. Serve cold with a topping of Special Mayonnaise (see recipe).

This is a later phase recipe.

Orange Aspic

1 envelope gelatin
2 tablespoons cold water
1½ cups orange juice
2 to 3 drops lemon juice
1 small can whole baby beets
(drained)

1 sliced ripe banana
1 small can white cherries
(pitted and drained)
½ cup heavy cream, whipped

Soften gelatin in cold water. Heat orange juice and add gelatin and lemon juice. Let cool until it begins to set. Pour a little into each of 2 individual molds, and add beets, banana, and cherries so that they are evenly dispersed in the aspic. Add the rest of the aspic and chill for at least 2 hours. Serve with whipped cream, which may be lightly salted. Makes 2 servings.

This is a later phase recipe.

Nectar Aspic

1 envelope gelatin
2 tablespoons cold water
1½ cups pineapple-pear nectar
1 (3 -oz.) package cream
cheese

2 tablespoons Special
Mayonnaise (see recipe)
½ cup diced, cooked, or
canned peaches (drained)

Soften gelatin in cold water. Heat pineapple-pear nectar and add gelatin. Let cool until it begins to set. Mash cream cheese with mayonnaise until thoroughly blended. Pour a little of the aspic into each of 2 individual molds, add ½ of the peaches to each and ½ the cream cheese mixture. Cover each mold with rest of aspic and chill. Makes 2 servings.

This is an early phase recipe.

Prune Aspic

1 envelope gelatin	1 ripe banana, sliced
2 tablespoons cold water	½ cup diced cooked dried fruit
1½ cup prune juice	(drained)
2 to 3 drops lemon juice	

Soften gelatin in cold water. Heat prune juice and add gelatin and lemon juice. Let cool until it begins to set. Pour ½ the aspic into a small mold and add the banana and cooked fruit. Add the remaining aspic and chill thoroughly. Serve with Special Mayonnaise (see recipe). Makes 2 servings.

This is an early phase recipe.

FISH SALADS

Cod and Avocado Salad

Toss ½ cup cold flaked cooked cod with ½ diced peeled ripe avocado and 3 tablespoons Special Mayonnaise. Makes 1 serving.

This is an early phase recipe.

Salmon and Egg Salad

Toss ½ cup flaked cooked fresh salmon with a chopped hard-cooked egg, 2 tablespoons oil, and 1 to 2 drops lemon juice. Makes 1 serving.

This is a later phase recipe.

Fish and Carrot Salad

Mash ½ cup diced leftover poached fish with ¼ cup diced cooked carrot and 3 tablespoons Special Mayonnaise. Mash until very fine. Use as sandwich filling. Makes about 1 cup sandwich filling.

This is an early phase recipe.

DESSERTS

The lover of sweet, rich, bland foods enters here into a special paradise. We have a total disregard for calories throughout our diet and here, if taste so dictates, we can really "go wild."

Many of these desserts are also food for between-meal snacking. We can and should indulge ourselves in creams, iced and otherwise, in custards, certain fruits, cookies, plain cakes, and so on and on.

In no other culinary area do we have such freedom or abandon, so if you have a sweet tooth, make up for the lean years now.

Stewed Dried Fruits

Prunes, raisins, currants, cherries, apricots, pears, and apples may be stewed, singly or in combination. The same method applies for all of them. The dried fruits are always available in sealed boxes. If there are shops in your area that specialize in fruits, nuts, and imported candies, they are well worth patronizing. They may sell the unboxed dried fruits which may be larger, fresher, and softer than the packaged, and have much more flavor. The stewed fruit will keep for several days in a covered bowl in the refrigerator, so for time-saving, cook a large quantity to have ready to serve. I find that if I mix a few different dried fruits and cook them a long, slow time, I can add more than the usual amount of water and have extra fruit juice from my fruit, and not sacrifice the flavor.

To cook:

Wash and drain bulk diet fruit. Cover with water. Simmer slowly at least 30 minutes. You can flavor the fruit with a thin slice of lemon cooked with it and later discarded. Taste for sweetness when the fruit is cooked, add sugar, if necessary, to taste.

GELATIN DESSERTS

Any of our fruits or juices can be used with unflavored gelatin or the prepared gelatin mixes. Gelatins are easy to prepare, they keep well, and are a nourishing food, contributing both sugar and protein.

Orange-Peach Gelatin

1 envelope gelatin
2 tablespoons cold water
1 cup orange juice

¼ cup sugar
2 medium peaches, peeled
and sliced

Soften gelatin in the cold water. Heat orange juice with sugar, and add gelatin, stir until dissolved. Let cool and begin to set. Arrange peaches in small mold and pour the gelatin over them. Chill. Makes 1 or 2 servings.

This is an early phase recipe.

Sanka Parfait

1 envelope gelatin
¼ cup cold water
¼ cup sugar

3 teaspoons Sanka instant
coffee
1½ cups boiling water
1 cup heavy cream

Soften gelatin in cold water. Heat sugar and Sanka together in hot water until sugar dissolves; add to gelatin. Pour into bowl and chill. Before it is completely set, whip 1 cup of heavy cream and when almost stiff add gelatin mixture and continue to whip. Spoon into parfait glasses, chill. Makes 4 to 6 servings.

This is a later phase recipe.

Rice Pudding, Fancy

1 cup cooked rice	3 eggs, beaten
½ cup sugar	⅛ teaspoon salt, or less
½ teaspoon vanilla	2 tablespoons white seedless
1 cup milk or light cream	raisins (optional)

Mix all the ingredients and pour into a deep 1½-quart baking dish. Bake in a moderate, 350° F., oven 35 minutes, or until custard is set. Serve warm or cold with cream or whipped cream. Makes 4 to 6 servings.

This is an early phase recipe.

Fruit Sauce for Ice Cream

1 pound dried Bing cherries	1 cup water
2 cups water	1 cup sugar
½ cup sugar	

Simmer cherries in 2 cups water with ½ cup sugar for 1½ hours. Boil 1 cup each water and sugar together 5 minutes. Purée cherries and liquid through food mill and add to sugar syrup, cook together 1 minute. Pour into several small jars, let cool, cover with tightly fitting covers. Store in refrigerator. Makes 4 to 8 small jars.

This is an early phase recipe.

PUDDINGS

Vanilla, chocolate, tapioca, and many other packaged pudding and "filling" mixes are available. For all these, and for junket, follow directions on the package. Avoid strange mixtures and, of course, the ones with nuts.

Rice Pudding, Plain

½ cup rice	⅛ teaspoon salt, or less
1 quart milk	1 teaspoon vanilla
½ cup white or brown sugar	3 tablespoons butter

Mix all ingredients except butter in a deep 1½-quart baking dish. Bake in slow oven, 250° F., 3 hours stirring occasionally. Add the butter at the start of the third hour, and stir for the last time. Serve warm or chilled, with cream. Makes 4 or more servings.

This is an early phase recipe.

Pound Cake

2 cups and 2 tablespoons
sifted all-purpose flour
¼ teaspoon salt
½ pound butter (2 sticks)
1 cup sugar

5 egg yolks, well beaten
½ teaspoon vanilla
5 egg whites, beaten stiff
Buttered paper

Sift the flour and salt together twice. Cream the butter and gradually add the sugar, beating until the mixture is fluffy. Add the
beaten egg yolks and continue beating until the mixture is very
light. (A rotary beater or electric mixer is good for this.) Sift in
the flour a little at a time beating constantly. Stir in the vanilla
and fold into the stiffly beaten egg whites. Pour into a buttered
9-inch loaf pan lined with buttered paper. Bake in slow, 300° F.,
oven 1¼ hours, or until it tests done. Let cool in pan 5 minutes.
Then turn out and let cool on cake rack. To store, wrap completely
cooled cake in heavy waxed paper or foil. Makes 12 or more servings.

This is a later phase recipe.

Angel Food Cake

10 egg whites	1¼ cups confectioners' sugar
¾ teaspoon cream of tartar	⅛ teaspoon salt
1 cup sifted cake flour	1 teaspoon vanilla

Beat egg whites until foamy, add cream of tartar and beat until stiff but not dry. Sift the flour, sugar, and salt together 4 times. Fold carefully into the beaten egg whites 2 tablespoons at a time, folding until mixture is smooth. Add vanilla and continue folding until well mixed. Pour batter into ungreased 9-inch tube pan. Bake in moderate, 325° F., oven 30 minutes, reduce heat to 250° F. and bake 30 minutes more. Remove from oven and invert pan on a standing bottle or upturned funnel. Let cake hang until cool. Remove from pan. Makes 8 or more servings.

This is an early phase recipe.

Chocolate Mousse

½ pound semi-sweet
   chocolate bits
½ cup sugar
¼ cup water

5 egg yolks, well beaten
1 teaspoon vanilla
5 egg whites, beaten stiff

Melt chocolate, sugar, and water in top of double boiler. Stir until it is very smooth. Place pan in cold water to cool chocolate. Add egg yolks and vanilla to cooled chocolate and blend. Fold mixture into stiffly beaten egg whites. Pour the mousse into 4 custard cups or a small mold and chill thoroughly. Makes 4 servings.

This is a later phase recipe.

CUSTARDS

Cooked Custard

4 egg yolks
4 tablespoons sugar

⅛ teaspoon salt, or less
2 cups hot milk

Beat egg yolks in top of double boiler, add sugar and salt, and continue beating until well blended. Put the pan over hot water and gradually add the hot milk, stirring constantly. Cook until the mixture coats a spoon. Pour into 4 custard cups, let cool, then chill. Makes 4 servings.

This is an early phase recipe.

Baked Custard

3 eggs   ⅛ teaspoon salt, or less
½ cup sugar   2 cups hot milk

Beat eggs, add sugar and salt. Add milk slowly and mix well. Pour into 4 custard cups, set them in a shallow pan containing about 1 inch of hot water. Bake in a moderate, 325° F., oven 30 minutes. Let cool, then chill.

This is an early phase recipe.

Variations:

1 3-oz. square of baking chocolate or 1 tablespoon instant Sanka may be added to the hot milk and blended into the custard.

Caramel Cream

2 cups light cream   ½ cup sugar
½ teaspoon vanilla   ½ cup boiling water
3 eggs, 2 egg yolks   1 cup sugar

Scald cream with vanilla. Beat eggs, extra yolks, and sugar, add scalded cream gradually, stirring constantly. Melt 1 cup sugar in a heavy skillet, carefully add boiling water, and boil until it is dissolved and brown. Coat a 1-quart mold or bowl with the caramel, pour in the custard and place it in a pan containing about 1 inch of hot water. Bake in a moderate, 375° F., oven about 45 minutes, or until a silver knife inserted in the center comes out clean. Let cool, chill, and unmold. Makes 4 to 6 servings.

This is an early phase recipe.

Bavarian Cream

1 envelope gelatin
2 tablespoons cold water
4 egg yolks
½ cup sugar

1 cup hot milk
½ teaspoon vanilla
1 cup heavy cream

Soften the gelatin in the cold water. Beat the egg yolks and sugar together until smooth in the top of a double boiler. Add the hot milk and vanilla and place over boiling water. Stir until the mixture is smooth and thick. Add the softened gelatin and blend until it is dissolved. Remove from hot water and let custard cool. Beat cream until stiff and fold into the custard, chill. Makes 4 servings.

This is an early phase recipe.

Use the egg whites (from Bavarian Cream) to make:

Meringues

4 egg whites, beaten stiff

1 cup sugar (half granulated, half confectioners')

Beat egg whites until stiff, add sugar and continue beating. Drop the mixture on a greased cookie sheet with a large spoon. Bake in a slow, 300° F., oven 10 minutes, reduce heat to 225° F., and continue baking 20 minutes longer. Remove and let cool.

This is an early phase recipe.

Gaufrettes (Cookies)

2 egg whites   ⅓ cup sifted all-purpose flour
½ cup sugar   3 tablespoons butter, melted

Beat egg whites until stiff, fold in sugar, fold in flour, fold in butter. Butter and flour a cookie sheet. Warm the sheet 2 minutes in a hot, 450° F., oven. Drop batter and spread thinly 1 tablespoon at a time on the cookie sheet. Bake 3 or 4 minutes until set and browning. Remove cookie sheet. Slip cookies off with spatula. Quickly roll each around knife handle or pencil. Let cool. Makes about 2 dozen.

This is an early phase recipe.

Fruit Cup

Ripe pears   Stewed dried fruits
Peaches   Bananas
Apricots   Cooked peeled apple
Canned white cherries   Orange juice

Any or all of the above, peeled and diced, may be combined with orange juice which will both flavor and keep the fruit from turning brown. The pears, peaches, and apricots should be very ripe.

This is a later phase recipe.

Peach Melba

1 large ripe peach
Boiling water
¼ cup water
½ cup sugar

2 drops vanilla
½ pint vanilla ice cream
Jelly (optional)

Drop the peach into boiling water for less than 1 minute. Remove from water and slip the skin off. Cut the peach in half and remove the stone. Boil the ¼ cup water, sugar, and vanilla together 5 minutes. Cook the peach halves in this syrup 10 minutes. Remove and let cool. Chill thoroughly. To serve, place each half peach, cut side up in a dish, fill the cavity with ice cream and, if desired, a tablespoon of jelly. Makes 2 servings.

This is an early phase recipe.

Baked Bananas (or Peaches)

1 ripe banana (or peach),
   peeled

1 tablespoon brown sugar
½ tablespoon butter

Split banana lengthwise; cut peach in half and remove stone. Mix sugar and butter and spread cut surface of fruit. Press together again and wrap loosely in metal foil. Bake 15 minutes in moderate, 350° F., oven. The fruit may be baked on the grill of a charcoal broiler; if this is used, turn the fruit twice, about every 5 minutes. Makes 1 serving.

This is a later phase recipe.

Peach Sorbet or Sherbet

This dessert is made basically of simple syrup and fresh fruit purée. It is served in stemmed glasses with a splash of a liqueur made of the same fruit. We will have to omit that final touch for the time being.

1 cup sugar	4 large ripe peaches
1 cup water	1 teaspoon lime juice

Boil sugar and water together 5 minutes. Set aside to cool. Drop peaches into boiling water 1 or 2 minutes, remove, and slip skin off. Cut into pieces and purée in blender with lime juice. Mix with sugar syrup and place in an uncovered bowl or tray in the freezing compartment of the refrigerator for about 4 hours. Do not stir mixture, it will freeze into a granular slush-like consistency. To serve, beat, and spoon into sherbet glasses. Makes 4 servings.

Other fruits from our list may be used in the same manner.

This is a later phase recipe.

Dessert Soufflé

3 tablespoons butter	½ cup sugar
2 tablespoons flour	1 teaspoon vanilla
1 cup milk	4 egg yolks, slightly beaten
¼ teaspoon salt	5 egg whites, beaten stiff

Butter a 1-quart soufflé dish. Melt butter, stir in flour and blend thoroughly. Add milk, keep stirring, and add salt, sugar, and vanilla. Cook until thick and smooth. Let cool slightly and beat in egg yolks, then fold into beaten egg whites. Pour the batter into the buttered dish and set in a shallow pan containing about 1 inch of hot water. Set the pan in a moderately hot, 400° F., oven. Bake 15 minutes. Reduce heat to 350° F., and bake 25 minutes longer. Do not open oven during the baking period. Serve immediately in baking dish. Makes 4 servings.

This is an early phase recipe.

Variations:

Chocolate Soufflé

Add 2 squares (1-oz. each) of baking chocolate, melted, to the butter-flour mixture, proceed as for Dessert Soufflé.

Coffee Soufflé

Add 1½ tablespoons instant Sanka dissolved in 2 tablespoons hot water to the butter-flour mixture.

Fruit Soufflé

Add ½ cup peach or other fruit purée when adding milk and sugar. Reduce sugar to ¼ cup, proceed as before.

Baked Apples

4 large baking apples	2 tablespoons butter
½ cup brown sugar (packed)	¼ cup graham cracker crumbs
½ cup orange juice	(optional)

Wash and core apples. Set in a shallow baking pan. Fill the cavities with brown sugar (and the graham cracker crumbs, if you use them). Moisten the sugar with orange juice and pour the rest of the juice into the pan. Dot the apples with butter and bake in a moderate oven, 350° F., 30 to 40 minutes. Apples can be baked with other food in the same oven and will adapt themselves to the cooking temperature of the other food. Makes 4 servings.

This is a later phase recipe.

Blender Pie

20 square graham crackers	2 whole eggs and 1 egg yolk
¼ cup brown sugar, packed	¼ to ½ cup sugar
¼ cup butter, melted	2 drops vanilla
1 cup applesauce	3 tablespoons seedless raisins
1 cup light cream or milk	or red currants (optional)

Break 2 or 3 graham crackers into blender container, cover and turn on to high speed until they are powdered. Empty the crumbs into a 9-inch pie pan and continue until all the crackers are crushed. Mix with brown sugar and melted butter and press into pie pan to make crust. Use a flat plate or another pie pan to press the dough into place.

Heat the milk or cream with the vanilla and applesauce. Beat all the eggs with the white sugar, add the sauce and raisins, and pour into the container of the blender. Blend for 1 minute. Pour carefully into the pie crust. Bake in a hot, 425° F., oven (preheated) 10 minutes, reduce heat to 350° F. and continue baking about 30 minutes, or until it tests done when a wooden toothpick is inserted. Let cool. Makes 6 servings.

This is a later phase recipe.

The graham cracker crust may be used with custard, fruit or other filling, and is our only "pastry."

Sponge Cake Roll

3 tablespoons sugar   3 eggs
3 tablespoons flour   1 egg yolk
1 tablespoon butter, melted

Beat the 4 egg yolks and sugar together until lemon-colored. Beat
the egg whites until stiff and fold in with the flour. Mix the
melted butter into the batter and spread on lightly buttered foil
or cookie sheet. The paste should be of a uniform thickness of
about ½ inch. Bake in a hot, 425° F., oven for 7 to 8 minutes.
Remove the cake to a flat surface (such as a marble top) and
cover with a towel and let cool. Cake may be filled with jelly or
whipped cream and rolled or dusted with powdered sugar and
cut into long "fingers." Makes 6 servings.

This is an early phase recipe.

Apricots Banville

6 canned peeled apricot halves   2 tablespoons powdered sugar
6 thin sugar cookies   Apricot syrup
½ cup heavy cream

Place the cookies on a flat plate and top each with an apricot half.
Whip the cream with the sugar and 1 teaspoon apricot syrup. Fill
each apricot with the cream and spoon apricot syrup over the
cream. Allow to chill thoroughly before serving. Makes 3 servings.

This is a later phase recipe.

Eggs in the Snow

3 egg whites	1 drop vanilla extract
3 tablespoons sugar	4 tablespoons sugar
2 cups milk	4 egg yolks

Beat egg whites and 3 tablespoons sugar until stiff. Heat milk and vanilla in a wide shallow pan until it boils. Drop egg whites in, a spoonful at a time, and poach without boiling for 2 minutes. Turn the whites in the milk with a fork and cook 2 more minutes. Drain the whites in a cloth.

Beat the egg yolks and 4 tablespoons sugar until thick, add to boiling milk that had been used to poach egg whites. Cook, stirring constantly until it is almost at a boil, then strain through a fine sieve into a shallow dish. Allow to cool and arrange the egg whites on the surface. Serve cold. Makes 4 servings.

This is an early phase recipe.

Pots de Crême Sanka

2 eggs
4 egg yolks
½ cup sugar

2 cup milk
1 drop vanilla extract
2 teaspoons instant Sanka

Beat the eggs, egg yolks, and sugar until thick and lemon-colored. Heat the milk, vanilla, and Sanka until boiling. Combine the mixture, let stand for a few minutes and fill custard cups or the little dishes called "pots de crême." Stand them in a shallow baking pan filled with boiling water and bake in a moderate, 350° F., oven for 20 to 30 minutes or until a knife inserted in the center of a custard comes out clean. The number of servings and the timing are dependent on the size of your containers. Serve chilled.

This is an early phase recipe.

MENUS FOR THE DIETER

Early Phase Menus

BREAKFAST

At home: Stewed peaches. Blender meal II. Sanka or Postum.

At home: 2 ounces orange juice with 2 ounces warm water. Coddled eggs. Toast and butter. Milk and Postum.

At home: Cream of wheat with maple sugar. Toast and butter. Sanka or Postum.

At home: Banana omelet. Toast, butter, jelly. Milk.

Restaurant: Basic blender meal. Toast and butter. Sanka.

Restaurant: 2 poached or coddled eggs. Toast and butter. Milk.

LUNCHEON

At home: Cream of pea soup. Cold poached breast of chicken on buttered toast. Milk or Sanka.

At home: Oyster stew. Soda crackers. Stewed pears. Sanka.

At home: Cream of avocado soup. Broiled chicken livers. Toast and butter. Sanka or Postum.

At home: Broiled chopped steak. Baby food spinach purée. Toast and butter. Milk.

Restaurant: Broiled chopped steak. Baked potato. Toast and butter. Milk.

Restaurant: 2 poached eggs on buttered toast. Milk shake.

Restaurant: Sliced white meat of chicken on buttered toast. Soft ice cream. (Plain flavors, such as vanilla, chocolate, no nut or fruit flavors). Sanka.

DINNER

At home: Cream of carrot soup. 2 broiled rib lamb chops. Baked potato. Custard. Sanka or Postum.

At home: Small glass of diluted orange juice. Creamed cod. pastine. Cooked carrots. Fruit gelatin. Sanka.

At home: Slice of ripe avocado, no seasoning. Broiled *filet mignon.* Buttered noodles. Purée of spinach. Caramel cream. Sanka.

At home: Broiled breast of chicken. Mashed potatoes. Purée of green peas. Angel food cake. Milk or Postum.

Restaurant: Small glass of diluted orange juice. Broiled chopped steak. Boiled potato. Custard or soft ice cream. Sanka or milk.

Restaurant: Slice of ripe avocado, no seasoning. Broiled steak fillet. Baked potato. Gelatin dessert. Milk or Postum.

Later Phase Menus

BREAKFAST

At home: Blender meal III. Toast and butter. Sanka.

At home: Stewed prunes. Shirred eggs. Toast and butter. Dry cereal and cream. Sanka or Postum.

At home: Sliced ripe peach, peeled. Unfried eggs. Toast and butter. Milk.

Restaurant: 2 poached eggs on buttered toast. Cereal and cream. Sanka or Postum.

Restaurant: Stewed prunes. Loose scrambled eggs. Toast and cottage cheese. Milk or Postum.

LUNCHEON

At home: Cherry soup. Salmon and egg. Crackers. Milk or Sanka.

At home: Chicken liver omelet. Bread and butter. Milk.

At home: Chef's salad. Hard roll and butter. Milk.

Restaurant: Beet borscht with raw egg. Broiled sole. Boiled potato. Soft ice cream. Sanka.

Restaurant: Small glass tomato juice. Cottage cheese and canned peaches. Crackers. Plain cake. Sanka or milk.

Restaurant: Sliced hard-cooked egg on buttered bread. Double rich milk shake or malted milk.

DINNER

At home: Potato soup. Salmon omelet. Sugar cookies. Milk or Sanka.

At home: Egg à la Russe. Baked stuffed bluefish. Ripe pear, peeled. Sanka.

At home: Cream of water cress soup. Broiled chicken with orange sauce. Carrot-potato puffs. Meringue. Sanka.

At home: Stuffed mushroom caps. *Mousse au Cervelle.* Gaufrettes. Sorbet. Sanka.

Restaurant: Small glass of fruit juice. Roast beef, no seasoning or gravy. Mashed potatoes. Cooked carrots. Soft ice cream. Sanka.

Restaurant: Slice of ripe avocado, no seasoning. Broiled calf's liver. Freshly cooked spaghetti with melted butter. Caramel cream, flan, or other custard. Sanka or milk.

Restaurant: Small glass of tomato juice. Broiled salmon or halibut. Baked potato. Chocolate cream pie — eat filling only, do not eat crust. Milk or Sanka.

MENUS FOR PREPARATION STAGING

The previous section lists meals exclusively for the dieter; this section sets forth menus that can be followed for family dining and for meals shared when one entertains guests. The suggestions show a pattern that makes the dieter feel part of the pleasant ritual of dining in company and can demonstrate the order of PREPARATION STAGE COOKING.

From the pre-dinner cocktail through the dessert and beverage the dieter enjoys a sense of participation. I found this far pleasanter than eating my bowl of gruel in company and then sitting back and following a conversation over food I could not share. After a while I could forget that my diet was so limited if I had something that approximated someone else's something. I reasoned that if one person drank soda water and another martinis, and a third a highball, why not enjoy the diluted orange juice. Not everyone eats each thing that is served. Some eat salad, some potatoes, and so on. If I could have part of what was served, then the meal became a brighter experience for all the diners.

MENUS FOR PREPARATION STAGE COOKING

single * see recipe — double ** see non-dieter recipes

EARLY PHASE

Dieter	Together	Non-Dieter
Diluted orange juice		Cocktails
Crackers and cream cheese		Peanuts, smoked oysters
	Cream of pea soup*	
Poached breast of chicken*		Chicken curry**
	Steamed rice*	
	Steamed carrots*	
Toast and butter		Hot rolls
	Caramel cream*	
Sanka or milk		Coffee

Dieter	Together	Non-Dieter
Avocado with Special Mayonnaise*		Jellied consommé
	Cod in egg sauce*	
	Mashed potatoes*	
Creamed spinach* (can be baby food)		Avocado and endive salad
Toast and butter		French bread
Orange-peach gelatin*		Fresh fruit in wine
Sanka or milk		Demitasse

Dieter	Together	Non-Dieter
Diluted fruit juice		Cocktails
	Chopped chicken livers* and crackers	
	Cream of asparagus soup*	
Broiled chopped steak*		Meat loaf**
String bean purée		French string beans
		Herb toast
	Angel food cake*	
Sanka or milk		Coffee

Dieter	Together	Non-Dieter
	Cod and avocado salad*	
	Jellied vegetable consommé*	
Sliced breast of chicken*		Chicken spaghetti sauce**
Spaghetti and butter*		Spaghetti
	Peach Melba*	with liqueur
Sanka or milk		Coffee

Dieter	Together	Non-Dieter
	Cream of vegetable soup*	
Broiled lamb chops*		Lamb casserole**
Mashed potatoes and carrots*		Tossed salad
Toast and butter		Onion rye bread
	Fancy rice pudding*	
Sanka or milk		Coffee

LATER PHASE

Dieter	Together	Non-Dieter
Diluted orange juice		Cocktails
Dry cereal*		Mixed nuts
	Cream of mushroom soup*	
Broiled steak*		Roast beef hash**
Baked potatoes*		Braised celery
Spinach purée* (can be baby food)		
Toast and butter		Hot rolls
	Blender pie*	
Sanka or milk		Coffee

Dieter	Together	Non-Dieter
Tomato juice		Bloody Mary's
	Mashed avocado* and crackers	
	Cherry soup*	
	Charcoal broiled chopped steak*	
	Baked potato*	
Baked beets*		Broiled ears of corn
Toast and butter		Garlic bread
	Baked bananas*	
Sanka or milk		Coffee

Dieter	Together	Non-Dieter
	Beet juice borscht*	
with sweet cream		with sour cream
Basic omelet		Eggs with vegetables**
Toast and butter		French bread
Asparagus purée		
	Pound cake*	
Soft vanilla ice cream		Ice cream
Sanka or milk		Coffee

Dieter	Together	Non-Dieter
	Fish bisque*	
Chef's salad*		Vegetable curry**
Herb butter* and	Steamed rice*	
	Baked apples*	
Toast and butter		Hot biscuits
Sanka or milk		Coffee or tea

Dieter	Together	Non-Dieter
	Cream of water cress soup*	
Broiled chicken livers*		Chicken livers and string beans**
String bean purée		
	Baked potatoes	
Toast and butter		Hot rolls
	Peach sherbet*	
Sanka or milk		Coffee

Dieter	Together	Non-Dieter
Avocado and Special Mayonnaise*		Shrimp cocktail
	Hot vegetable consommé*	
	Baked stuffed bluefish*	
	Carrot-potato puffs*	
Tomato aspic*		Tossed salad
Toast and butter		French bread
	Chocolate mousse*	
Sanka or milk		Coffee or espresso

Dieter	Together	Non-Dieter
	Tomato bouillon*	
	Creamed sweetbreads*	
Boiled new potatoes*		French fried potatoes
	Small steamed early peas*	
Toast and butter		Hot biscuits
Sanka parfait*		Fruit pie
Sanka or milk		Coffee

RECIPES FOR THE NON-DIETER

This section is for the rest of the ulcer patient's family. The recipes are leftovers or parts of the food that the dieter should avoid. It embodies my principle of PREPARATION STAGE COOKING.

I hope that the ideas it sets forth will aid the family cook and point a direction to follow, both in the marketing and the preparation of food. Each recipe uses as its basic ingredient the foods cooked or partially prepared for the special diet. The meat, chicken, and vegetables have been cooked without seasoning and in a quick, simple fashion. It lends itself to speedy conversion into other simple, tasty dishes and avoids costly waste of food and time. Another important factor is that the family will eat essentially the some foods in the same meal.

Eggs with Vegetables

6 eggs, beaten with a little water	Bacon, ham, or other meat
2 to 4 ounces butter	Sliced peeled tomatoes
Leftover cooked vegetables (potato, carrot, beans, etc.)	Sliced onion or chopped scallions
	Diced cheese

This recipe is to be varied according to taste and supplies. If bacon is used cut it into small pieces and pan broil it, drain the fat and add the tomato, onion, and other vegetables. Cook them for a few minutes, adding butter as needed, a little at a time. Add cheese and pour eggs over the whole of it. Reduce heat, cover pan and cook slowly until the eggs set and puff slightly. Cut pancake with a spatula and serve immediately. Makes 2 or 3 servings.

Chicken Pot Pie

1½ cups diced cooked chicken
  1 cup diced cooked
    vegetables
  4 to 6 steamed mushroom
    stems, minced
  1 cup light cream sauce
    made with chicken stock

1 ounce dry vermouth or
  sherry
Salt
Pepper
Pastry or bisquit dough

Line a deep pie plate with the pastry dough, reserving half for the top crust. Mix all ingredients into the cream sauce and pour into the pie. Arrange the top crust and cut slits to allow steam to escape. Brush top crust with a little milk and bake in a moderate, 375° F., oven for 30 minutes. Makes 2 or 3 servings.

Chicken Spaghetti Sauce

1½ cups diced cooked chicken
  ½ cup chicken stock
  1 medium onion, minced
  1 green pepper, chopped
  4 peeled and sliced
    beefsteak tomatoes

Salt
Pepper
Basil or tarragon
Garlic

Combine all ingredients, excepting chicken, and season to taste. Cook at a low boil for 20 minutes. Add chicken and cook for 10 minutes longer. Makes 4 servings.

Creamed Chicken

2 cups diced cooked chicken
1½ cups cream sauce
1 teaspoon paprika
1½ ounces dry vermouth or
   sherry

1 teaspoon each parsley and
   chives, finely chopped
Salt
Pepper

Add all the ingredients to the heated cream sauce and cook for 5 minutes. Serve on toast points or over rice. Makes 4 servings.

Chicken Livers and String Beans

1 pound chicken livers,
   coarsely chopped
2 pounds string beans, frenched
   or 2 (8-ounce) packages
   frozen string beans

1 medium onion, minced
3 tablespoons butter
Salt and pepper to taste

Steam the string beans and set them aside. Sauté the onion in the butter until it is clear, add the chicken livers and continue cooking, stirring often, until done. Season with salt and pepper and toss with the string beans. Add more butter if necessary. Makes 4 servings.

Chicken Curry

2 cups diced chicken, cooked
2 medium onions, chopped
2 stalks celery, chopped
1 green pepper, chopped
1 tablespoon curry powder

3 tablespoons oil or fat
Salt
Pepper
2 cups chicken stock or milk

Sauté the vegetables in the oil until they are very soft. Add the chicken and sauté for a few more minutes. Add the curry powder, salt and pepper and the stock or milk. Cook over medium heat for 15 minutes. Serve with rice and favorite condiments. Makes 4 servings.

Meat Loaf

1½ pounds ground meat (may
   be mixture of round steak
   and chuck)
2 slices bread, soaked in
   water
1 small onion, minced

Salt
Pepper
1 egg
1½ ounces sweet vermouth
1 (8-ounce) can tomato
   purée

Mix and blend thoroughly all ingredients, but only half of the tomato purée. Pack into a loaf pan and pour second half of the tomato purée over the meat. Bake in a medium, 350° F., oven for 40 minutes. Serve hot or cold. Makes 4 servings.

Steak Tidbits with Mushrooms

1½ pounds steak, cut into medium cubes	2 tablespoons sherry
½ pound mushrooms, cut in halves	3 tablespoons oil
1 tablespoon minced shallots	Salt
4 tablespoons soy sauce	Pepper
	Dry mustard

Make a marinade of all the ingredients and thoroughly coat steak and mushroom pieces with it. Place this in a covered bowl in the refrigerator overnight. Mushroom stems and steak trimmings from the dieter's food may be used for this dish. The heart of a large steak could be cut out and the rest of it cut into cubes. Broil the steak and mushrooms under high heat for 5 minutes, turning and basting them twice. Makes 4 servings.

Lamb Casserole

4 large shoulder lamb chops
2 large potatoes, peeled and
  diced
2 medium carrots, peeled and
  sliced
1 medium onion, sliced thinly
1 large peeled tomato or 1
  (8-ounce) can solid-pack
  tomatoes

1½ ounces dry vermouth or
  sherry
Salt
Pepper
1 teaspoon Worcestershire
  Sauce (optional)

Arrange lamb chops in the bottom of a covered casserole. Cover with vegetables, arranging them in the order given. Pour wine and seasonings on last, cover and bake for 1 hour in a moderate, 350° F., oven. Makes 4 servings.

Roast Beef Hash

2 cups diced cooked roast beef
1 cup diced cooked potato
1 small onion, finely minced
Salt
Pepper

2 tablespoons catchup
  (optional)
¼ cup beef stock or strong
  consommé

Chop all ingredients except for beef stock together until fairly fine and well blended. Set in refrigerator to chill. At serving time, heat stock in skillet, place meat mixture into it and press down with spatula. Cook over medium heat for 5 minutes or until thoroughly heated. Makes 4 servings.

Hamburger Pie

1½ pounds ground meat   2 tablespoons oil
  2 cups mashed potatoes with   Salt
    1 egg   Pepper
  1 cup chopped onion, celery,
    green pepper and
    mushroom stems

Sauté the cupful of chopped vegetables in the oil until soft. Arrange the mashed potatoes in a baking pan to form a bottom crust. Spread the vegetable mixture over the potatoes, season and place the meat, formed into 4 cakes, on the vegetables. Bake in a hot, 450° F., oven for 15 to 18 minutes. Makes 4 servings.

Vegetable Curry

½ cup each chopped onion,
   celery, green pepper
1 cup peeled diced apple
Minced garlic
   1 tablespoon curry powder
   3 tablespoons vegetable oil

3 tablespoons seedless raisins
Salt
Pepper
Powdered ginger
2 cups milk, heated

Sauté the onions, celery and green pepper in oil until soft. Add the apples and cook for a few minutes, stir in the seasonings and raisins. Add the hot milk and cook for 20 minutes at a simmer. Serve with rice, condiments, and tiny meatballs simmered in a little beef stock.

EARLY PHASE RECIPES

LATER PHASE RECIPES

INDEX